Items should be returned on or before the last date
shown below. Items not already requested by other
borrowers may be renewed in person, in writing or by
telephone. To renew, please quote the number on the
barcode label. To renew online a PIN is required.
This can be requested at your local library.
Renew online @ **www.dublincitypubliclibraries.ie**
Fines charged for overdue items will include postage
incurred in recovery. Damage to or loss of items will
be charged to the borrower.

Leabharlanna Poiblí Chathair Bhaile Átha Cliath
Dublin City Public Libraries

Baile Átha Cliath
Dublin City

| Brainse Rátheanaigh |
| Raheny Branch |
| Tel: 8315521 |

Date Due	Date Due	Date Due
	27 JAN 2017	
2 2 JUL 2014	30th March	2 4 NOV 2016
1 9 SEP 2014		
2 3 NOV 2015		0 7 MAR 2015
0 9 NOV 2016		2 3 FEB 2016
20/12/16		0 5 OCT 2016
		0 3 APR 2018
		1 0 JUL 2019
		20 NOV 2019

In My Own Light

A Memoir

Raymond Deane

The Liffey Press

Published by
The Liffey Press Ltd
Raheny Shopping Centre, Second Floor
Raheny, Dublin 5, Ireland
www.theliffeypress.com

A catalogue record of this book is
available from the British Library.

ISBN 978-1-908308-57-3

Printed in Spain by GraphyCems.

Contents

For Renate Debrun
and
In memoriam Declan Deane (1942-2010)

Prologue

Beginning is not only a kind of action. It is also a frame of mind, a kind of work, an attitude, a consciousness.

– Edward Said

The paragraphs that follow were culled from my medical records of July 1987, kindly provided by St. Vincent's Hospital after I had completed most of this memoir. Reading them a quarter century after the emergency they describe was more harrowing than writing about them (in Chapter 27 below). The photocopied handwritten and typed pages were somehow more tangible than memories, and of course they contained references to much that I could not remember, was not aware of at the time, and now could barely decipher.

ﺵ   ﺵ   ﺵ

St. Vincent's Hospital
Elm Park, Dublin 4

Re: <u>Raymond Deane, ** Upr. Leeson St., Dublin 4.</u>

This 34 year old man was admitted as an emergency at 17.15 on 8th July 1987. He had an epileptic fit and was transferred to Casualty comatose, feverish, with abnormally low blood pressure and a severe metabolic acidosis (pH 6.9, bicarbonate 5.9). He admitted to heavy alcohol intake, 10 pints per day until shortly before admission. While in the Accident and Emergency Department, he required aggressive resuscitation with intravenous sodium bicarbonate, empirical intravenous antibiotics

3

and control of super-ventricular tachycardia with intravenous Verapamil.

He had previous admissions to hospitals in Dublin with alcohol related disease. He seemed to have an isolated social background.

ON EXAMINATION

He was tremulous, shaky, fine tremor, no nystagmus. Cardio-respiratory examination was unremarkable. His liver was enlarged by two finger-widths. Abdominal examination otherwise was unremarkable. There was no peripheral oedema. Neurological examination was normal. Fundi were clear.

CLINICAL IMPRESSION

Clinical impression was of a severe metabolic acidosis, probable lactic acidosis post epileptic fit. There was also a history of heavy ethanol intake and the fit could well have been part of a withdrawal syndrome. Liver biopsy revealed abnormality in the lobules taking the form of extensive fatty degeneration of hepatocytes. These appearances are those of severe steatosis. No evidence of hepatitis, of granulomatous disease, or of cirrhosis was present.

COURSE IN HOSPITAL

He was managed as outlined above. Over the subsequent 24-48 hours he became increasingly agitated requiring Hemineverin (chlormethiazole) infusion. He was reviewed by our Psychiatric colleagues who agreed with the diagnosis of alcohol related delirium tremens. Two or three days after admission he became unrousable due to excess sedation. His airway was compromised and he was transferred to

Intensive Care Unit for closer monitoring of his airway.

With intravenous vitamins, antibiotics and a progressive reduction in his sedation there was marked improvement in his clinical status over the subsequent week. Prior to discharge he was reviewed by Dr. **** *******, Consultant Gastroenterologist, who agreed to follow him in Outpatients with respect to any possible hepatic sequelae of his heavy ethanol intake. Prior to discharge ultrasound of liver, spleen, pancreas and a gastroscopy were normal. He was discharged on 22.7.87. on a regime of Orovite and Thiamine.

PSYCHIATRIC COMMENTS

15 years of alcohol abuse,

Several previous episodes of DTs.

Previous admission to St Brendan's 1979 - very short and no follow-up.

History of alcoholism on both sides of family.

Personal history:

Composer and concert pianist.

Left school at 14 and self-educated from then on.

Did very well at college and given several awards.

Recent traumas: break-up with live-in girlfriend of 3½ years and mother's death last year.

Currently in rented accommodation.

Has commissions.

```
Contrite.

Willing to seek help.

No significant affective illness.

No psychotic features.

? truly insightful.

Discussed options for treatment of alcoholism
and he will consider them.

Basically a loner with no close friends.
```

Of course, those final words resonate dolefully, but more disturbing is the enigmatic '*? truly insightful*'. At first I took this for a compliment, but a psychologist friend has translated them as meaning 'I do not think he has much insight into his condition'!

How did I reach such a point of no return? And how did I come eventually to move on after all and build a productive life for myself?

I embarked on this memoir in an attempt to answer these questions, and am by no means certain that I have succeeded. In the course of writing, however, I came to see the attempt in a different light: as more descriptive, perhaps, than analytical, although I have attempted here and there – and above all in the Epilogue – to engage in some tentative analysis. I make this point lest fellow-sufferers from the condition of alcoholism should seek here some kind of key ('*truly insightful*') that might unlock the gate of recovery. This I cannot do, but I can describe how one hopeless drunkard stumbled through that gate, thus proving that there is no such thing as a hopeless drunkard.

Music has been central to my life, and for this reason I have been obliged here and there to employ mildly technical terminology. The reader to whom this is incomprehensible need not worry about skimming these passages judiciously.

Throughout I repeat as a refrain: *this is not a misery memoir!* My childhood was not bleak and loveless. Neither, I should add, is it *an alcoholic memoir*, a mere case study. The word 'alcoholic' does not denote some kind of essence that encapsulates and reduces the integrity of the alcoholic's experience, before, during and after (if it is accurate to speak of 'after' in this context) the onset of addiction.

If nothing else, I hope that this book may prove a talisman against fatalism.

ڪ   ڪ   ڪ

Part One

Childhood is not only the childhood we really had but also the impressions we formed of it in our adolescence and maturity.

– Cesare Pavese

Chapter 1

My mother was a peripatetic child-bearer: each of her four surviving children was born in a different hospital, in a different part of the country. To facilitate my arrival on 27 January 1953, she chose a nursing home in Tuam, County Galway, run by the Bon Secours Sisters, affectionately known as the 'bone-suckers'.

The circumstances of my birth disqualify me from claiming Achill as my birthplace, but my first few unconscious days hardly qualify me as a Galwegian. These fine distinctions – the two counties rub shoulders and a couple of hours' drive separate Tuam from Achill – are of considerable importance in Ireland. But of course Achill is where I was brought up and must have played a major role in making me whatever it is that I have become.

Achill is separated from the mainland by a 200-yard bridge named after Michael Davitt, one-armed hero of the late nineteenth century land wars. I often tell people, usually gullible foreigners, that I was brought up on an island off the coast of an island off the coast of an island (Great Britain) off the coast of a continent. But whereas the mythology of such western islands as Aran inevitably evokes storm-tossed journeys by frail *currach* with attendant fatalities and posthumous keening,

Achill, excessively accessible, doesn't feel like much of an island at all.

The village of my upbringing is called Bunacurry, and is situated in the centre of the island. Whereas the bulk of the village was officially designated a *Gaeltacht* or Irish-speaking region, the 'high street' where we lived belonged to the *Galltacht* (*gall* = foreigner). In reality, most denizens of this particular *Gaeltacht* had retained just as much of their native language as secured them the sum of £5 sterling per annum, bestowed on the recommendation of a *Cigire* (Inspector) who never troubled to probe too deeply the linguistic skills of those who entertained him during his annual flying visit with cups of tea and lamentations about the weather – for which a very minimal vocabulary sufficed.

In those years the island was an impoverished place, although it had been lent a certain mystique by the Belfast artist Paul Henry (1876-1958) who painted many evocative land- and seascapes there in the second decade of the twentieth century. Some years later, in 1954, the great German novelist Heinrich Böll visited the island and conveyed his impressions in his *Irisches Tagebuch (Irish Diary)*. Although not free from a certain romanticising tendency, the book gives a vivid image of life in pre-contraceptive rural Ireland, alongside moving reflections on the phenomenon of emigration that was then a defining feature of Irish life. Böll's cottage, exquisitely situated in Dugort under the protection of Slievemore mountain, has since been turned into an artists' residence.

An earlier temporary resident of the island with an eye for a seascape was Captain Charles Boycott. Perhaps he should have remained in Corrymore House with its spectacular views of sea and cliffs instead of moving to the mainland in 1877 as estate agent to the Earl of Erne. It was there, near Ballinrobe, that he got into a spot of trouble with Charles Stewart Parnell, 'the uncrowned king of Ireland', who recommended that the Captain's tenants should punish him for his colonial ruthlessness 'by putting him in a moral Coventry, by isolating him from the rest of his country as if he were the leper of old...' The Captain's name was transferred to the tactic that drove him out of the country, and the term 'boycott' was born.

The house that my maternal grandfather John Connors built is called The Grove, and is situated on Bunacurry Crossroads, also known in his honour as Connors Cross. As ever, reality is refractory and this crossroads is merely a T-junction of the main thoroughfare with a secondary road leading to The Valley, Dooniver and Dugort.

John Connors was a Waterford man who at some point changed his name from O'Connor to Connors in a curiously pointless anti-nationalist gesture. This decision would rebound against him when he found that the Connors were a prominent clan among the local 'tinkers' or travelling people in Mayo, and hence the name had a different social stigma attached. My mother, who resented the name-change, liked to claim this unintentional elective kinship as a badge of honour.

John O'Connor/Connors had been an officer in the predominantly Catholic Royal Irish Constabulary (RIC), the British police force during the years of occupation. Throughout the 1918-21 War of Independence the loyalty of its members was severely tested, many choosing to collaborate with the IRA rather than work alongside the bloodthirsty British recruits known as the Black and Tans. Not so my grandfather, who according to one legend helped train these nasty characters in Dublin. The truth, rather less unsavoury, seems to have been that he trained RIC recruits in what was called 'gunnery', or the handling of firearms.

When the Irish Free State attained independence in 1922, it is hardly surprising that John Connors was one of those officers of the now disbanded RIC forced to leave the country. He took his wife and children into exile in Liverpool. This, even if something of an Irish ghetto, must surely have been an inhospitable environment for my Anglophobic mother. On returning to Ireland a few years later, John retreated to his wife's native county (she was an O'Malley from near Westport), purchased six acres of land, and built a two-story house that, for its time and place, was handsome to the point of ostentation. The homestead was adjacent to Lough Naneaneen *(Loch na n'Éinín* – Lake of the Little Birds), a modest expanse of water that I regarded as 'ours', although we didn't actually own it.

John had two daughters, my mother Mary Josephine and the much younger Patricia. Surviving photographs show that Patricia was a beauty very much in the film star mould of the era, while my mother was on the plain side. In 1944, aged 24, Patricia succumbed to tuberculosis, a disease that wreaked havoc in Ireland until its eradication by Dr Noel Browne in the 1950s. Apparently my grandfather was influenced by the contemporary prejudice that saw this affliction as some kind of disgrace, and refused to provide Patricia with the medical attention that might have saved her life. This, at any rate, was the accusation levelled against him by my mother, who never forgave him for the death of a sister she clearly idolised.

In addition, my mother was fiercely nationalistic, and regarded her father's former profession as a source of undying shame. Of her two younger brothers the easy-going Jim may or may not have shared her views in this respect, but Jack undoubtedly went to the other extreme: he joined the Royal Air Force and became a minor war hero when in 1945 a troop of Italians surrendered to him in the Tunisian desert. Jack compounded his crimes by being an atheist, living in England, and eventually becoming an ardent Thatcherite.

My grandmother, Nora Connors, taught in Bunacurry girls' primary school, of which she would eventually become principal. A former pupil described her as 'a quite particular but a very good teacher' and 'quite the Victorian schoolmarm, lace collar and all'. My mother, less Victorian in demeanour but equally so in values, would teach in the same school and also become principal.

She first encountered my father at a dance in the Parochial Hall at Achill Sound, where he approached her masquerading as 'a detective from Dublin', spinning a cock-and-bull story about her parked car having aroused his suspicions and thereby luring her outside for a chat. Such quirky, fantastical humour was very characteristic of him, and clearly was the correct note to strike with the deceptively demure spinster.

At that time Donald Patrick Deane worked as a civil servant in the Department of Social Welfare (the Labour Exchange) in Achill Sound. More than a decade earlier he had spent some time in the Christian Brothers. He had also taught for a time in either Ballybofey or Stranorlar in County Donegal, in the northwest. He had little to say about this period, but I believe that he lodged in one of the 'twin towns' and taught in the other, and in cycling between them was obliged to dismount from his bicycle and walk past a particular haunted field, so severe was the fit of involuntary trembling that seized him in its vicinity.

He now lived in a rented room above Ted Lavelle's pub near Cashel, a village between Bunacurry and Achill Sound. World War II – euphemistically known in Ireland as 'The Emergency' – had just broken out, and it was known that in his room the handsome Kerryman listened to wireless broadcasts from

Germany in the sinister tongue of that country. One evening he received a note containing the very stilted German words *'Wollen Sie mit mir spazieren gehen?'* ('Do you wish to go for a walk with me?'). The author of this coy query was Mary Josephine Deane, the walk took place, to be followed shortly afterwards by an engagement.

My mother received advice from all quarters – including her brother Jack, no paragon himself – that the wild civil servant with the mop of fair hair was a little too partial to the bottle, a little unreliable, perhaps a little crazy, and should be avoided like the plague. A streak of contrariness in her nature responded to similar traits in his, and well-intentioned advice merely served, as so often, as a stimulus to take the opposite course.

ڪ   ڪ   ڪ

I had little exposure to my father's side of the family, with the exception of his eldest sister Margaret and her offspring, in particular my cousin Jerry (Jeremiah) who lived in London but always came to Achill during his regular visits to Ireland. The family's roots were firmly planted in the beautiful Dingle peninsula in County Kerry.

Between Tralee – the capital of Kerry – and Dingle there is a tranquil and somewhat melancholy valley called Gleann-na-nGealt, which means 'the valley of the mad'. This apparently casts no aspersions on the mental health of its inhabitants, but refers to the curative qualities of water in a well situated in the valley. Gleann-na-nGealt is supposedly where Mad Sweeney, a legendary mediaeval king of Munster, found refuge when he was banished to wander Ireland for a year and a day.

Gleann-na-nGealt was the home turf of my great-grandparents, John Deane and Anne Cash. From here, the family moved to a handsome farmhouse outside the nearby village of Camp. This house still exists, is still handsome, and is still inhabited.

Through my paternal great-grandmother I am distantly related to Thomas Ashe, a follower of the socialist revolutionary James Connolly, and predecessor of Michael Collins as leader of the Irish Republican Brotherhood. Having participated in the abortive 1916 rising, Ashe died in Dublin's Mountjoy prison as a result of his hunger strike and the measures of forced feeding to which his jailors resorted. Collins delivered the oration at his funeral.

Apparently the Deanes and Ashes fell out over something or other, most likely that most popular bone of contention in rural Ireland: a right of way.

From Camp, the Deanes moved to Clandouglas, a rather featureless townland near the equally featureless town of Lixnaw. Here their son Jeremiah, my great grandfather, taught in the national school, of which the principal was a Mr Brosnan. Jeremiah married the latter's daughter, Mary Josephine, and took over as principal on her father's retirement.

By the time Mary Brosnan died of tuberculosis in 1915, aged thirty-six, she had given birth to no fewer than 10 children. Two of these, Denis and Mary Josephine, died in infancy and are buried alongside their parents in Kilfinnehy cemetery, under a headstone sculpted by Jeremiah himself. He was an enthusiastic stonemason who built several houses in the neighbourhood, including his own, and sculpted many headstones, also including his own. Because of the sandstone he used, many of these headstones have crumbled. Those that survive are of an idiosyncratic and somewhat kitschy style, with a crucifix frequently surmounting a stone in the shape of a heart inscribed with a great deal of Gaelic writing in different colours.

Teacher, classicist, linguist, bee-keeper, traditional musician and master builder, Jeremiah Deane was clearly a formidable character. In surviving photographs he invariably wears a forbidding aspect, and I recall my father often referring to his severity. My late brother Declan once made a pilgrimage to Kilfinnehy where he encountered an elderly man who had known 'Master Deane' and was full of praise for him. Asked if Master Deane had any faults, he reluctantly conceded that 'he might have had a mind for the dhrop', a predilection for alcohol that has dripped persistently down successive generations of our family.

Mary Brosnan's eldest child, my Aunt Margaret, lived with her argumentative and sardonic husband Luke, a former policeman from County Monaghan, in the village of Shillelagh, County Wicklow. In these idyllic surroundings I spent the only two unaccompanied holidays of my childhood days. During the first of these I was repeatedly reduced to tears at the dinner table by Luke's stern admonition to 'go aisy on the sugar – it's all we have in the house!' Eventually Cousin Jerry took me aside and explained that the old man was only teasing me, and that the best way to respond was by ignoring him and helping myself to even more sugar. I was reassured, but cannot recall whether I took his advice.

Aunt Margaret was present, along with my sister Patricia and myself, at our mother's deathbed in a hospital in County Wexford on Christmas Eve, 1986. Our father had just left the ward to attend evening mass. The startlingly depleted figure on the bed had long departed the world of consciousness, and, judging by her frowning features, was struggling with troublesome issues beyond our ken. Suddenly, shockingly, our 85-year-old aunt sprang with unsuspected agility to her feet and pinched Mary Josephine's nostrils between thumb and index finger. A connoisseur of extinction, she had been alert to its arrival in the case of my mother, and had hastened to prevent the issue of any disagreeable matter from her nose. However, for a ghastly instant it appeared to my sister and me as if Margaret had suddenly decided to terminate her sister-in-law's agony. She herself lived lucidly and lovingly until the eve of her 99th birthday.

ﺵ　　ﺵ　　ﺵ

When my parents married in 1940 they came to live with John Connors in The Grove. Predictably, this was anything but a harmonious arrangement. For one thing, my father was every bit as ardent a republican as my mother. For another, their attempt to import a dog into the ménage was met with a resolute veto. Neither side being prepared to compromise, the young couple plus dog moved out again and rented rooms in a house a quarter mile down the road, behind the girls' school. My grandmother, a gentle and accommodating soul, can hardly have enjoyed this situation, but no doubt the feud kept our neighbours entertained.

By the time my eldest brother Declan arrived in 1942 the quarrel had been patched up and the whole family, with or without the controversial pet, resided in The Grove. Apparently the subsequent arrival of grandchildren John in 1943 and Patricia in 1949 softened the crusty and authoritarian character of the patriarch, and at the end of his life my siblings recall him as a benign presence. John Connors died in his late seventies in March 1953, two months or so after my birth. His widow lived on for another thirteen vague and amiable years.

As soon as they finished primary school, each of my brothers in turn was sent to board at Mungret College, Limerick, an institution run by the Jesuits. In accordance with the most deeply-held desire of every Catholic Irish parent, it was understood that the first-born son would progress from there directly to the priesthood. At a later date my mother would temporarily come to regard the Jesuits as little better than a gang of communists, but for the time being Declan's acceptance by the world's most prestigious Catholic order was a source of unalloyed pride.

Not to be outdone, my brother John 'entered' the Holy Ghost Fathers after leaving Mungret. Fortunately for the posterity of the Deane family line he changed his mind in due course, and emerged to beget three delightful daughters by two successive wives.

The age gap between myself and my brothers and their absence at boarding school during my early childhood meant that I felt like an only son. Three times a year, during holiday periods, I would briefly be reunited with two boisterous strangers who treated me with affectionate if patronising brusqueness and then disappeared just as suddenly. So grown-up did they appear to me that I saw them more as uncles than as brothers, although the levelling effects of passing time restored the sense of fraternity.

Between their visits, there was my sister and her strange girlish universe, and beyond that a baffling outside world that I approached with excruciating timidity.

Chapter 2

In an essay on Kafka, Walter Benjamin referred to photography studios that were 'somewhere between a torture chamber and a throne room'. What I believe to be my first memory is of precisely such a studio in Westport, the nearest comparatively large town to Achill. My proud parents had taken me there, aged three, to be photographed.

The photographer, an old gentleman (as I perceived him) in a grey suit, seated me on an uncomfortable wicker-chair. To distract me, he handed me a miniature gnome or leprechaun with a faintly disagreeable, rubbery texture. I knew that I would not be allowed to keep this thing, so it merely heightened my sense of sullen resentment while not alleviating my anxiety. The real cause of both emotions was total ignorance as to what was happening, or why it was happening.

The photographer steps behind an antiquated mechanical contraption, his face concealed beneath a black cloth. Suddenly, he is a monster, a human torso with a head like a giant black insect. He calls on me to smile, his voice muted, barely human. My mother also urges me, but I cannot, will not, smile. When the camera flashes I begin to weep and it is all that I can do not to drop the toy and flee.

Many years later I rediscovered this photograph in a cache of old snapshots belonging to my cousin Jerry. I was astonished to find that my facial expression is anything but woebegone, indeed it is almost gleeful. And yet I was so certain of the version with which I had been living for so long that I could clearly see in my mind's eye the glum *moue* of which I had written!

And then came the next shock: in the same cache of photographs, I encountered one taken a year or two after the session in Westport. My hair is still more or less blond, although I no longer have my long curls. I am wearing the distinctive expression for which my family adopted the powerful adjective *wirrasthroo* (a corruption of the Irish *A Mhuire, is trua,* or *O Mary, 'tis a shame*). I had transposed the wistful frown from the later image onto the shy grin of the earlier one, and modified my memory of the photographic session accordingly. I have no idea what passing catastrophe had caused my sadness in the later snapshot.

That I had deceived myself about the nature of my very first memory (if such it truly was) is worrying. Naturally, this makes me wonder how many details of other memories have been fabricated by a later need to find explanations, even justifications, for inexplicable behaviour. This may be simply a definition of autobiography.

ڝ   ڝ   ڝ

Perhaps no man is an island, but for a child a house can be an island and for me The Grove was Achill.

The house was of no particular architectural distinction, but was and is a striking, yellow building commandingly situated on the aforementioned Connors Cross.

The grove in question consisted mainly of pine trees planted by my grandfather. Naturally enough, the modest dimensions of this wood were no obstacle to its becoming in turn the Black Forest, Sherwood Forest, the Forest of Arden, or whatever legendary plantation I happened to encounter in the course of my obsessive reading. At night it became the repository of dark forces, unknown but not unimaginable, a place which nothing would have induced me to enter.

Apparently the patch of land in which my grandfather had planted this grove was nothing but a sandpit, and because of its exposed position was known poetically as *'claisín na gaoithe'* ('the sandpit of the winds'). He had laid down a foot and a half of soil, which eventually proved an inhospitably shallow bed for some of the larger trees. In the legendary storm of 1993, one of these fell its full length, destroying part of the boundary wall and indeed knocking off a corner of the house itself.

The ground floor consisted of sitting room, dining room, maid's room, and kitchen. The dining room was mostly where family life took place. It had two windows, one facing the grove, and the other overlooking the main road. Beyond that was The Village, which acquired utopian status for me simply because my parents forbade me to visit it. Beyond that again was the bay with its little harbour. Beyond that again was Ballycroy, a name with all the magic of Shangri-la. Much of my time was spent tucked up in the window seat, my attention shifting from the book, comic or sketchbook in my hands to the remote landscape across the water, or – just as often – to the mist and rain blocking it from view.

The harbour boasted a pier – or 'quay', rhyming with 'grey' – jutting into the Sound. Although I observed this pier every day when it was not obscured by mist, I left Achill without ever having visited it. Deciding that a mere prohibition did not provide sufficient deterrence, my parents saw fit to add an extra bundle of warnings: between the road and the seafront there was a treacherous stretch of bog, the sands of the tiny beach were soft and treacherous, the tide came in quickly and treacherously, everything about the place was treacherous, as treacherous as memory itself.

Forty-five years later, on a warm, sunny but showery day in May 2008, I at last walked 'down the village' to the quay.

The first revelation was that the village was a pleasant enough place, distinguished only by the unusual absence of any kind of public house or café. It consisted of a single un-pretentious street barely meriting the name, rather than the Dickensian labyrinth that I had visualised.

The second was that the quay was so much further away than it had seemed – perhaps two miles, rather than a few hundred yards.

The third was that there was no sulphurous bog and no quicksand, and that the harbour itself had the feel of a rather benign place, hosting a handful of trawlers and motor boats.

With hindsight I marvel at the abject mixture of obedience and cowardice that kept me from breaching my parents' prohi-bition. My siblings claimed that they were at liberty to visit the village and quay at will, and that they frequently did so. Perhaps the prohibition was imposed exclusively on myself because I was a solitary child, and would have been at risk of drowning had I been allowed to explore the harbour unaccompanied.

I have ever since been fascinated by harbours, and above all by the beauty of piers. Perhaps they embody the lure of for-merly forbidden territory?

ﺱ   ﺱ   ﺱ

The dining room of The Grove was dominated by an open fire-place with a hob (a stone seat) on either side.

Majestically seated on one of these, Nana (my grandmoth-er) would read her daily newspaper – the *Irish Press* or *Irish Independent,* depending on the shifting political allegiances of my parents – concentrating mainly on the obituaries, which seemed on a daily basis to include at least one former acquaintance. Her unfailing placidity, only very occasionally yielding to a touch of sarcasm, meant that she was scarcely considered as part of the hierarchy of authority within the household. Her presence resembled that of a well-loved if rather substantial pet, if not a living, breathing and often humming piece of furniture. I marvelled at her ability to maintain her post on the hob despite the often overpowering heat emerging from the turf fire, which she tended with the patience and gentleness that characterised all her actions and transactions. She was fond of intoning drawing room ballads in a soft high-pitched voice, her fond, watery eyes fixed on a nebulous inner distance:

> *Where I sported and plaaayed*
> *In a green leafy glaaade*
> *By the banks of my own lovely Leeeee...*

Each evening at nine o'clock a space would be cleared in front of this fireplace for the family rosary, a ritual in which I was included only once I was old enough to be up at that hour. My first awareness of the rosary, therefore, was of a mysterious but somehow reassuring buzz rising through the floorboards, prefacing my father's goodnight visit with its attendant bedtime story.

These stories came from remarkably disparate sources. Sometimes they were tales that he himself had heard in his childhood from the *Seanchaí* (traditional Irish storyteller) William Hennessy. Sometimes they were freely derived from ancient Irish sagas like the *Táin bó cúailgne (The Cattle-raid of Cooley)* and concerned such heroes as Cúchullain, Ferdia, and (my favourite) Caoilte MacRónán Na Scéil (Caoilte-son-of-Ronan-of-the-stories).

Most entrancing of all were those which he read from well-thumbed little volumes in Russian script, for he had maintained and extended his interest in foreign languages since his marriage, despite the withering contempt his wife displayed, or had come to display, for such futile enterprise. These tales included 'Taman' and 'Bela' (the latter presumably somewhat expurgated) from Lermontov's *A Hero of our Time* and, best of all, *A Prisoner in the Caucasus* by Tolstoy.

Another tale, German this time, was delightfully entitled '*Schnuppeldiwupp*', by one Fritz Halbach. Its full title is '*Schnuppeldiwup: Eine Geschichte für Kinderherzen*'. 'A Story for Childish Hearts' sounds very appealing, yet I can remember nothing about it. Perhaps this lack of distinguishing features explains why neither book nor author has stood the test of time – or perhaps it is the *Kinderherzen* that have vanished.

Another German story was 'Immensee' by Theodor Storm. Decades later the train in which I was travelling from Basel to Locarno in Switzerland came to a halt in a station called, to my great delight, Immensee. Although I could remember nothing of the story, I was thrilled to think that this exquisite alpine region had some notional link to my distant past.

When I got around to reading Storm's story for myself, I found that its setting could not possibly have been in Switzerland, that the story was strong on idyllic atmosphere and symbolic imagery but short on narrative, and that my father had supplied most of the latter out of his own head. Nonetheless, the story had served briefly to endow with enchantment a provincial Swiss location that, for all I know, may well deserve it.

Very occasionally, my father would turn his attention from Russian and German authors and recite from memory Robert Browning's poem 'How They Brought the Good News from

Ghent to Aix', or 'The Jackdaw of Rheims' by the more obscure Richard Harris Barham:

> *The Jackdaw sat on the Cardinal's chair!*
> *Bishop and abbot and prior were there...*

This delightful narrative poem culminates in the cheeky jackdaw being canonised 'by the name of Jem Crow!'

This mixed bag of stories and poems served to familiarise me from an early age with some of the greatest and more obscure names of world literature, and ensured that I never had a sense that such writing belonged to an elevated sphere outside of the range of ordinary people.

Chapter 3

'You always have your nose stuck in a book!' was a phrase that I heard with equal frequency from my mother and grandmother. The former quite simply disapproved of books, unless the author was a Catholic fanatic or Agatha Christie. Nana was perennially worried that I was sitting 'in my own light', that is to say, with my head between the light – be it natural or artificial – and my reading or writing material.

My other favourite activity, which also took place in the dining room, was drawing. My passion for this may have suggested to onlookers that I had a talent for graphic art, but my primary interest, as I recall it, was narrative. In effect, I drew comic strips without speech bubbles. Depending on what pulp I had most recently been devouring, the subject matter veered between chivalry (in its militaristic rather than romantic aspects), cowboys and Indians, and World War II.

The dining room boasted a large radio on which the names of the various stations, most of them unlinked to any intelligible reception, were a source of mystery and fascination. Stavanger, Spitzbergen and Hilversum acquired a character and aura derived entirely from the sonority of these weighty trisyllables plus a few sparse images derived from Arthur Mee's *Children's Encyclopedia*: massive rusty oil tankers, cranes, girders and derricks looming into perpetually dark skies, gloomy bearded men in long oilskins, wheeling and screeching terns and kittiwakes, whales surging majestically from dark roiling deeps...

Radio Éireann was the only station to which our parents encouraged us to listen, confident as they were in those days that no proprieties would be breached by our infant national broadcaster. The news and weather forecast, sports results, horse racing and football matches were the principal items on the listening menu. Entertainment was provided by a soap opera called *The Foley Family*, its interest heightened by the fact that my mother had somehow become acquainted with a couple of its cast members during her years at Carysfort teacher training college in Dublin. I found it incomprehensible, and was particularly alienated by the exaggerated Dublin accents affected by its characters. However I loved the theme music which I much later discovered to be a piece called *Le Jet d'Eau* by Sydney Smith, a once popular English composer of salon piano music, surely a most inappropriate choice under the circumstances.

Inevitably, however, the innocence of our listening habits became contaminated. As my sister and I grew older we discovered pop music, and we persuaded our reluctant parents to let us listen every week to the Irish Top Ten. They hated this stuff, of course, in particular the real or simulated American accents of the singers, and the concentration on what my father somewhat unkindly derided as 'calf love'. Our discovery of Radio Luxemburg was a particularly hard blow for the parents and grandparent, and our access to it was strictly rationed.

From the start I worshipped Cliff Richard and an Australian singer called Frank Ifield, who for some reason specialised in yodelling, surely an accomplishment not much prized in the outback. I sought to develop this technique with such application that my distraught father at last asked me to desist, pointing out that the only fit place for such sounds, if such a place existed, was the wide open spaces of the Alps.

However, I was encouraged to memorise a couple of songs as party pieces. One of these was Marty Robbins's hit *The Hanging Tree*. Although I loved this song dearly, I came to loathe performing it for my parents' guests on account of the references to 'my own true love' which invariably produced knowing smirks from the audience and mortified blushes from myself.

Another of my songs also had an arboreal connection: *The Fairy Tree* had been recorded by my mother's favourite singer, John McCormack, and had the advantage of a religious theme, the tree in question being the one from which Christ's crown of thorns was made. The song had the twin benefits of satisfying my mother's religiosity and my own partiality to ghost and fairy lore, inclinations that are of course closely linked.

My repertoire was completed by *Faraway Places (with strange-sounding names)*, a former Bing Crosby hit of which a version by an Irish trio called The Bachelors became popular in the early 1960s. I didn't much like the song itself, nor the singers (they didn't even yodel), but its words filled me with yearning for China, Siam and castles in Spain.

Not long before we left Achill the radio was supplanted – or supplemented – by a black and white television set, one of the first to make an appearance on the island. At the time there was a vogue for American dramas featuring escaped criminals or/and lunatics who knock on the doors of remote farmhouses seeking a drink of water, directions to the big city, or the use of a telephone. No sooner is the menacing psychopath allowed inside by the gullible housewife, who seems impervious to the sinister background music, than a knife is produced, the unfortunate lady is gagged and tied up, and unimaginable – or all too easily imaginable – horrors ensue.

Around this same period, the village was agog when a local man called Pat S. went insane. He cornered the curate in his presbytery and threatened him with a bread knife stolen from the clerical kitchen. The terrified but resourceful priest, normally a sedate and dignified man, managed to elude him and fled up the road clutching his soutane above his knees, pursued by the knife-wielding maniac, a sight unseen that I often replayed in my imagination. Eventually Pat S. was captured before anybody came to any harm, and bundled off to Castlebar mental hospital.

This incident, coupled with the rash of pathological TV shows, had a traumatic effect on me. I became afraid to go unaccompanied to the upstairs lavatory at night, and refused to sleep on my own in the room I had shared with Patsy before she went to boarding school. I was moved into my parents' bedroom, thus interfering with whatever lingering inclination towards intimacy they might still have possessed, and became seriously prone to bed-wetting.

ۍ   ۍ   ۍ

If the dining room was the scene of everyday life, the sitting room was designed for more specialised pursuits such as piano practice and the reception of visitors. Its most conspicuous furnishings were a large bookcase and an upright piano. The latter would loom large in my life, but also to some degree in the lives of my siblings, each of whom was obliged to engage with its mysteries.

The bookcase had glass doors and sat atop an enclosed cabinet containing, among other treasures, the Dansette gramophone and the vinyl records it was designed to play. The books belonged, mostly, to my father and testified to his status as a rural intellectual with ideas above his station. There were classic texts in German, French and Russian, as well as secondary literature concerning the history of these cultures, all underlined and annotated in my father's spidery script.

My mother, although an inveterate Anglophobe, considered that after Shakespeare the only truly great literature had been written by the English romantic poets. She could quote at length from Shelley, Keats, Wordsworth and Alfred Lord Tennyson. She would concede certain virtues to the early work of W.B. Yeats, given that although nothing but a Protestant he was nonetheless a kind of patriot. However, she probably had reservations about his morals and would have found much of his later verse both obscure and obscene.

Neither of my parents insisted that my reading should focus on Irish authors. They probably were less than overjoyed that I became addicted to such quintessentially English schoolboy fodder as Richmal Crompton's *Just William* books, Enid Blyton's *Famous Five*, Charles Hamilton's *Billy Bunter* series so admired by George Orwell, and – worst of all – W.E. Johns's tales about the heroic fighter pilot James Bigglesworth, known to his chums as Biggles, a sworn enemy of 'the Hun' and friend of the gallant British Empire. Nonetheless, no serious attempt was made to curb these tastes, particularly as I had also acquired a liking for the more acceptable Charles Dickens, having read *David Copperfield* unabridged at an absurdly early age.

Also on the ground floor was the maid's room. Since most of our maids lived nearby, this small and basic bedroom was rarely inhabited. Its window served me as a shortcut from the back yard into the house, since every little boy considers it more honourable to enter a house by a window than by a mere door.

It may appear somewhat aristocratic of us to have boasted the services of a maid, but both my parents worked full time and away from home. In my memory the maids, none of whom remained with us for more than a year or two, were all called Mary or Ann, or perhaps Mary Ann (there may have also been a Brigid). I vividly recall Nana one afternoon calling in her pleasant sing-song for refreshment with the words 'Mary – another sup of tea please, Ann!'

I was encouraged to be civil to these young women, and indeed had little sense that they were servants or minions. While they spent much of their spare time in the kitchen, they would occasionally join us for afternoon tea and engage in cheerful gossip with my grandmother or mother, if the latter had returned from school. My mother had a powerful sense of moral responsibility in their regard, of course, which manifested itself in her constantly plying them with Catholic Truth Society leaflets on various moral issues.

Did the CTS also publish the little biographies of saints that occasionally turned up in the house? I particularly remember the tale of Father Damien, or Saint Damien of Molokai (1840-1889), who, although not canonised until 2009, had long been regarded as the patron saint of lepers. This booklet contained a particularly vivid account of how Damien, whose ministry was carried out in Hawaii, was scalded when he accidentally spilled a pot of boiling water over his hand but felt no pain. *He said nothing about it* (this detail seemed particularly striking and ominous), but realised that he had himself contracted leprosy, the disease that would eventually kill him.

For some time after reading this hair-raising narrative I periodically ran hot water over my hand to ensure that I was free of leprosy, an illness that, to the best of my knowledge, had never been endemic to County Mayo. Later on I took to examining the undersides of my arms for boils after reading a description of the symptoms of cholera, and later still, after my sister's circumstantial description of seeing some unfortunate person in the throes of epilepsy, I grew reluctant to take a bath lest I have a seizure and drown. Chronic hypochondria must be added to the growing list of anxieties that accompanied my development.

My mother was particularly persistent in pressing CTS pamphlets on our penultimate Achill maid, Anne H., no doubt because she was a highly attractive sixteen-year-old and hence more than usually at risk from the prowling village Casanovas. Anne came from Inishbiggle, a flat little island off the east coast of Achill that was not always easy of access; this meant that she occupied the maid's room.

When she arrived in The Grove I was nine, already quite conscious of the fact that girls were not merely defective boys, and aware of the fact that Anne was remarkably pretty, if at sixteen a little over the hill. In addition, she had a pleasant personality and related to me as one human being to another, something that I greatly appreciated. She shared with me her anxiety about her skinniness, and her confidence in a bottled remedy called Wate-On. I gallantly assured her that she had no need of it. Most impressively, she confided to me that she was being secretly courted by a neighbour's son; such trust in my discretion was surely reckless, as my mother's wrath would have been terrible had I blabbed.

ݽ   ݽ   ݽ

Between the sitting room and dining room, underneath the staircase, there was a tiny box room containing domestic utensils such as brushes, dustpans and an electric iron. There was no vacuum cleaner, an implement unheard of in rural Ireland at that time.

From the low sloping ceiling of this closet hung a straightened clothes hanger, which skewered my father's collection of receipts and unpaid bills. Every so often he would take out this menacing object and place it on the dining room table. He would don his reading glasses and, frowning and sucking through his teeth, remove bits of paper from it with one hand while jotting figures in a notebook with the other.

For me, watching in awed fascination, this clothes hanger represented everything that was terrifying about the prospect of becoming an adult and having *responsibilities*. Although that word was probably unknown to me as yet, the concept that it represented had acquired overtones of anxiety and oppression that it has never lost. When we moved to Dublin, a similarly situated closet housed another batch of baneful papers skewered on another straightened clothes hanger – or was it the same one, carefully packed and delivered the breadth of Ireland at the instigation of my economical mother?

ﺱ   ﺱ   ﺱ

The upper storey boasted four bedrooms and a bathroom. My parents' bedroom contained two double beds, one of which I shared, for a time, with my father while my mother slept in the other. I can only recall a single occasion when Dad crept between those other sheets and sounds of murmuring and kissing ensued – nothing more dramatic, no primal scene. On the other hand, I frequently observed my mother in the mornings as she washed herself before the mirror, using a jug and a basin of (cold?) water. On one occasion she noticed my gaze fixed on her ample breasts and informed me, to my considerable astonishment, that once upon a time they had nourished me.

This was the only 'fact of life' that was ever imparted to me by either parent, and I'm not certain that I lent it much credence.

Across the landing from this chamber was Nana's room, with its pervasive and permanent smell of powder mingled with urine. Periodically, from the large bed in which she spent much of her time, she urged me to open the top drawer of her dresser, remove a Calvita box (this was a brand of cheese that first came on the market in the year of my birth), and open it. I did so and was confronted with a profusion of golden curls, shorn from my head shortly after the time of the Westport photograph, and retained ever since by my sentimental granny. I would touch the downy stuff reverentially, remove a tress and, gazing in the mirror, hold it in the vicinity of my forehead, imagining myself as the cherub of yesteryear. Nana would gently command me to stop before I let any of the precious matter drop on the linoleum.

ڪ   ڪ   ڪ

Behind The Grove were the outhouses and garage. The outhouses were in fact a single building consisting, on the ground floor, of a turf-shed, a workshop, and a store room containing the staircase to 'the loft'.

The workshop was my father's special domain. From nails and hooks attached to the walls hung saws of various sizes. Other implements, nameless to me, were scattered on a worktable to which was attached a vice, into which I loved to insert pieces of wood which I squeezed until I could squeeze no more. Another device that exercised a particular fascination was a spirit level. The function of this was a total mystery to me (yet another one!), but I loved to tilt it to and fro and observe the movements of its imprisoned air bubble, which I fantasised was a living creature. Everywhere in this room, on the floor and benches and hovering in the dimly illuminated air, there was sawdust, and a mingling of carpentry smells – oil, resin, wood, leather – that combined to convey a peculiar magic entirely divorced from the practical purposes for which the room and its contents were intended.

Within this space my father habitually wore his inimitable expression of intent concentration – brows furrowed, lips stretched and parted, air sucked in between teeth clenching and unclenching as if chewing over a knotty problem, be it the establishment of a true horizontal, the appropriate definition of a Russian verb, or the evaluation of financial data skewered upon the straightened clothes hanger.

Unlike the compartmentalised ground floor, the loft was a single undivided space that lent itself to many uses, practical and playful. Its stone walls were hung with pictures of pastoral scenes – cows, sheep, streams, shepherds and fishermen. I loved these humble works dearly and lost myself in the atmosphere they evoked, somehow more tranquil and reassuring than the actual rural environment in which I lived.

My sister and a couple of her schoolmates once devised an evening's entertainment to be presented in the loft. There would be recitations and songs, Patsy would play the piano-accordion at which she had acquired considerable proficiency, and there would almost certainly be some Irish dancing.

Naturally I was filled with a mixture of contempt and envy at the prospect of these maidenly antics. I pleaded with Patsy to let me contribute something together with P.J. and Blond-ie, two rather older schoolmates of mine with whom I would frequently sit around on various fences discussing the affairs of the day. We were particularly exercised by the adventures of 'th'Irish in th'Cawngo', those Irish troops participating in a peacekeeping mission in the former Belgian Congo, several of whose number had been massacred by Baluba tribesmen at Niemba in November 1960. Did we even remotely understand anything about this appalling conflict? I doubt it very much, but for many years the term 'Baluba' was one of the blackest insults you could offer anyone you disapproved of.

Given that my two cronies and I had hitherto featured not at all in Patsy's plans for the evening, except perhaps as barely tolerated audience members, it is hardly surprising that she bitterly resisted this uninvited interference. My next tactic was to whinge to my parents about being excluded from the fun, upon which, although fearing the worst, they gently urged their daughter to relent. She did so with petulant reluctance and a prescient cry of 'you'll spoil everything!'

In those days feature films screened in Bunacurry Hall – a long low building with a corrugated iron roof a little way up the main road – were often coupled with shorts featuring The Three Stooges – Larry, Moe and Curly-Joe. These noisy, slapstick productions involved idiotic plots exhibiting a narrow range of boorish behaviour, and are now almost completely unwatchable. This was all the same to us young cinemagoers, who had no conception of any loftier form of comedy.

Hence, after an hour or so of well-rehearsed and well-behaved performances, there must have been a collective sinking of hearts when I announced that the next item would feature 'the Three Bunacurry Stooges'.

The backdrop to this item was provided by a broad chimney stack that bisected the loft about three-quarters way down its length and rose from a fireplace in the workshop beneath. This structure had a ledge on either side, about six feet from the floor. On one of these somebody, presumably my complicit father who possessed a broad enough streak of mischief to anticipate the ensuing disaster with silent relish, had at my request placed a schoolbag prior to the show.

The plot of my little drama entailed one of the Bunacurry Stooges pointing out the object to his mates as they sauntered past.

'What is it?' (pronounced 'Phwat ez et?') ...

'It's a ...'

This was the extent of the scenario I had devised, and what ensued was entirely improvised. The object, unmistakably a brown leather satchel, was successively identified as a gun, a duck, a corpse, depending upon what came into my head, my co-stars relying almost entirely upon my prompts. Our attempts to secure the mysterious object entailed a great deal of jumping and falling, climbing on chairs and falling, climbing on one another's backs and falling, a certain amount of pushing and shoving, and much shouting and noisy laughter – the latter from ourselves exclusively, not the embarrassed audience of family and neighbours and my unfortunate sister's school friends.

I cannot recall whether I had devised any dénouement to the spectacle, such as one of us finally retrieving the wretched bag and thereby provoking a disillusioned cry of 'it's only an oul' schoolbag!' I may indeed have placed some 'surprise' inside, the discovery of which would have required further pushing, shoving and guffawing. However, somebody – either my mother or grandmother – interrupted the performance with the dry observation that 'we've had enough falling around and shouting for now'. At this the relieved audience members applauded with mock gusto while the frustrated actors bowed awkwardly, perhaps not entirely convinced by either their own efforts or the simulated enthusiasm of the public.

Predictably, Patsy was on the brink of tears, and raged at the blundering little brother who had spoiled her lovingly prepared evening. It took several days for relative peace to be restored.

ک   ک   ک

During the day the grove lost much of its nocturnal menace but none of its magic, particularly once I had mastered the art of climbing some of the less intimidating trees. One in particular possessed an intersection of strong branches that seemed made to accommodate my backside, and I climbed it whenever I got an opportunity and the wind was not too strong.

I have a memory that I suspect is cobbled together from distinct occasions, but that is none the less vivid for that. It is a sunny, mild, only slightly breezy day. I am sitting in my lofty nook proudly peeling and eating an orange. The tree is swaying gently from side to side, a whispering emanates from the neighbouring trees swaying in sympathy, and the breeze carries an aroma of resin. From the monastery half a mile away the Angelus bell rings, and simultaneously a cuckoo strikes up from its perch in some distant thicket. I am Tarzan. Had I ever heard of him, I might have been Mad Sweeney of Gleann-na-nGealt, the king who thought he was a bird and grew feathers to prove it. Above all, I am happy, although I probably do not know it.

The fields to the left of the lake path were entirely unused except during harvest time, when neighbours helped us to 'save the hay' and majestic haystacks, now a thing of the past, rose miraculously from the stubble. On the right, there was an area of bogland on which, in profusion, grew a white, silky plant known as bog cotton. Its snowiness and fluffy texture reminded me of marshmallow. I would collect little bouquets of the stuff with which I would happily caress my cheeks before scattering it to the breeze, making sure that nobody witnessed such sissyish antics.

One day my mother's brother Jim was due to pay one of his rare visits. I was in a state of excited suspense – Jim was my godfather, had sent me a present for every one of my birthdays, and had endeared himself greatly to me (as he did to every-one) on a previous visit with his anecdotes and shanties. From the latter I can only remember a single highly expressive line, delivered with avuncular panache: 'I stuck her with my big penknife...' I raced to the boggy field and lovingly collected a bunch of bog cotton which I carefully tied together with a rub-ber band. Bearing this gift, I self-consciously stood alongside my mother awaiting the evening bus from Westport.

When the bus arrived, Uncle Jim tottered from it in a state of high inebriation. My mother's reaction was instantaneous and shocking. She ran to him, seized his shoulders, and shook him vehemently, hissing out the words, 'You're nothing but a *scut*, that's what you are, a *scut*!!' She pushed him, protesting mildly, past me into the house and up to the spare bedroom where, no doubt, she subjected him to a further merciless dressing down before insisting that he sleep it off before show-ing himself to the rest of the family.

Crestfallen and baffled, I removed the rubber band from my snowy bouquet and scattered the flowers onto the pine-strewn floor of the grove.

For several days there was an atmosphere of constraint in the household as my contrite uncle slowly charmed himself out of Coventry. His offering to me was a geometry set, con-tained in a handsome cedarwood box which I retained for a quarter century or so (I have no recollection of what became of it). Its contents were something of a disappointment, as they were neither edible nor was it possible to discharge them with a loud bang. Try as he might, Jim could neither initiate me into the mysteries of geometry nor interest me greatly in them, although I was fascinated by the device known as a compass. For some time my drawings of cowboys, Indians, and knights in armour were decorated, independently of narrative content, with perfect circles of various sizes.

During the summer, when traffic increased owing to the influx of tourists, I enjoyed standing in The Grove's gateway waving at the passing cars, at least one of whose occupants usually waved back.

At one point, my sister sought to persuade me that I should adopt the persona of a 'Teddy Boy', a phenomenon about which she may have been informed by our English relatives. In the wake of World War II, young Englishmen started modelling their mode of dress on that of Edwardian England, or at least on their possibly satirical notion of what that entailed. Eventually, Edward became Teddy, and once the mock-nostalgic fashion had melded itself to an obsession with American pop music, the Teddy Boy was born and rapidly acquired rebellious and violent connotations.

Although a Teddy Boy in short trousers was a bit of a contradiction, I made the best of the few resources I possessed. I took to Brylcreeming my hair and vigorously back-combing it in order to acquire a quiff, a fashion to which it offered determined resistance. I kept the collar of my jacket raised at all times. I chewed gum with studied nonchalance, and indeed made chewing motions even when no gum was available, occasionally interrupting my mastication to curl my lip Elvis-wise.

Learning that the Teds fought other gangs with bicycle chains, I removed the chain from my own bike and slouched for hours in front of the house, chewing, curling my lip, and threateningly swinging my oily weapon. I was convinced that this apparition struck terror into passing motorists, particularly the English ones who would immediately identify my uniform and slam down the accelerator.

The family dog was Laddie, a ginger-and-white mongrel of raffish habits and charm. Although companionable enough and promiscuously affectionate, he obviously considered his true home to be 'down the village', where he could consort and copulate with others of his kind. Sometimes he would disappear for days, then reappear in lamentable condition, smelly, bloodied, and not entirely unbowed – until such time as he had gathered strength for the next foray.

On one occasion my father locked him in the loft, convinced that this would dampen his ardour. Next morning he was nowhere to be found; somehow he had squeezed through the narrow aperture of a slightly-open window, had leapt from the second floor on to stony ground without sustaining injury, and had returned to his canine revels down the village.

This unsatisfactory situation might have continued indefinitely, had Laddie not developed a fatal interest in the chickens belonging to our neighbour Eddie, under normal circumstances a thoroughly biddable gentleman. Nonetheless, Eddie called a halt to Laddie's mischief after losing several birds to his cheerful greed, and convinced my reluctant father that the beast was beyond redemption and had to be slain.

Dad being unable to steel himself to perform this task, it was agreed that Eddie would come to The Grove, armed with his trusty shotgun, and do what was necessary.

Patsy and I cowered in the dining room, fully aware of what was happening in the back yard, yet under strict instructions neither to venture outside nor to watch through the window.

A shot rang out, followed by a shriek of canine agony, and intermingled cries of manly distress. We ran into the kitchen, but simultaneously the back door was pushed open and Laddie hobbled in and hid under the table, trembling and whimpering, a strip of torn rope hanging from one hind paw, one front paw shattered and bleeding. Weeping in anguish, we joined him under the table, throwing our arms around him while he licked our faces in a frantic and hopeless appeal for protection.

But adults, however kind-hearted, are inflexible. Our father was upon us a moment later, tearing poor Laddie from our feeble grasp and somehow dragging him back to the yard where a moment later Eddie successfully administered the *coup de grâce*.

Undoubtedly, I was shocked and grief-stricken by this appalling incident, and to this day my sister has blotted the more gruesome details from her memory. But I cannot recall nursing more than the most transient grievance against my beloved father, perhaps because he was himself so patently overwhelmed by the horror of it all. Even the inept marksman Eddie seems to have escaped becoming the object of any lingering resentment. Perhaps, when all is said and done, my attachment to Laddie, like his to me, did not run all that deep. I think of him as a dog's dog, and his patent lack of exclusive devotion to my needy and egotistical self evoked in me a correspondingly detached affection not unmingled with a touch of resentment.

ڪ   ڪ   ڪ

As for my English cousins, one thing was certain: they were *posh*.

They were not exactly English – their father was Irish and their mother Franco-Tunisian – and they quite possibly would not have been regarded as posh by a true-blue Englander. But to my ears, accustomed to the bog-patois of my schoolmates ('Phwat ez et!?') or the blandly neutral tones of my family, the English spoken by these girls was utterly exotic, sometimes comical, but quintessentially *posh* and hence fit to inspire feelings of inferiority and envy.

Uncle Jack himself, the RAF war hero and Tory sympathiser, exuded his own brand of poshness, although his accent was probably closer to Foxrock (a posh suburb of South Dublin) than Dorset, where 'the Jacks', as we crudely dubbed them, lived. He spoke in a kind of leisurely drawl, sported a pencil moustache, smoked a pipe, and exuded an aroma of good tobacco and aftershave. I'm sure that my mother was galled by his nonchalant manner, yet simultaneously impressed by and perhaps even proud of it.

As for Aunt Madeleine, whom Jack had courted in Tunisia, the scene of his RAF derring-do, I was completely captivated by her accent, her appearance, her manner. If posh Englishness was exotic, Madeleine represented exoticism infinitely multiplied. I was under the mistaken impression that she was an Arab – her mildly aquiline nose catered to whatever vague image of Arabness I had acquired from my scarcely reliable sources (*The Children's Encyclopedia* and comic books).

The two older cousins, Michelle and Patty, were much the same age as my sister and hence treated me with merciless condescension. This sufficed to arouse my prickly defensiveness, and blinded me to any more amiable qualities they might have possessed.

Their sister Aileen, however, was only a few months older than me. On the day of their arrival for their first visit during my lifetime I was entrusted with the task of 'showing her around', a case of the shy leading the reserved. She wore what in those days was called a 'costume', a matching jacket and skirt in some light colour. She wore her short auburn hair in a fringe that fell almost to the eyebrows that surmounted her brown eyes, and had about her a grave poise that I had never encountered in someone of my age, and that was missing from her more garrulous sisters.

I led her into the back yard and showed her the outhouses and the path to the lake, and must surely have ushered her into the wood, although I cannot recall this. In her presence I was completely disarmed of the swagger I might have assumed had she been a boy or a tomboy. I felt myself to be clumsy and awkward in the face of such quietude, and can hardly imagine that I distinguished myself by my conversational gambits, 'th'Irish in th'Cawngo' being unlikely to evoke much response.

Although my infatuation with the mysterious Aileen was entirely innocent, an unfathomable sense of guilt and shame attached itself to it – no doubt a sad side-effect of my puritanical upbringing.

Chapter 4

Bunacurry Boys' National School was run by the Irish Order of Friars Minor, better known as Franciscans. These good souls were popularly known as 'the monks', an inaccurate usage in that monks are monastically enclosed whereas friars are active in the world. Their monastery was located about fifty yards from the modest schoolhouse. It boasted a tantalising orchard – strictly out of bounds to schoolboys – and a tiny church whose bell rang tinnily thrice daily, a peaceful sound that, heard from afar, features prominently in my repertoire of aural memories.

'The monks' wore long brown cloaks tied at the waist by a length of rope, sporting cowls that I never recall being drawn over their wearers' heads. These garments made a whooshing noise when the brothers walked, and the entire ensemble was an inexhaustible source of speculation, inevitably centred on the question, 'what do they wear underneath?'. No aura of mediaeval mystique radiated from these earthy men, who were by and large a benevolent lot.

I was five years old when I started school. On my first day I was entrusted to the care of P.J. and Blondie, who would evolve into my fellow 'Bunacurry Stooges'. These were the sons of a widowed neighbour, were senior to me by several years, and were brawny enough to inspire confidence in my parents and fear in any schoolmates inclined to start bullying me from day one. This protective role appeared to embarrass them and their vigilance barely survived my first week at school, although we remained friends.

For the time being all was well, and I was quickly lulled into the deceptive sense that school was a home from home. The building itself consisted of just two rooms, housing 'the little lads' and 'the big lads' respectively. The latter consisted of Fourth to Sixth Classes which, when I started, were under the tutelage of Brother Angelo, a tall, thin man who reminded me of President de Valera. He had a reputation as a disciplinarian that seemed confirmed by the occasional explosions of vituperation thundering through the flimsy wooden partition, usually followed by up to six short sharp slaps and a deathly silence.

I was never taught by Angelo, but in my rare personal encounters with him I found him gentle and courteous, and he was reputed to be a man of real scholarship.

'The little lads' were divided into Baby Infants, Infants, and First through Third Classes. They were under the care of two brothers. It was quickly decided that I was too advanced for Baby Infants, where the tots were mainly preoccupied with weeping and sucking their grubby thumbs. In Infants we busied ourselves with modelling figures from plasticine (known as 'dhobe', presumably a corruption of 'daub'), learning the English and Gaelic alphabets, and memorising the eternal truths of the One True Faith from a little green-coloured Catechism. Since I could already read and write with some fluency, my rise through the ranks continued apace and in no time I was in First Class.

School finished at 3.00 p.m., upon which, at first escorted by my two gawky bodyguards, I would stroll home along the main road. All more adventurous routes through the fields or bogs were strictly forbidden by my parents.

Hitherto I had been a solitary child, unaware that other children had such things as playmates. If my parents believed that school would do anything to change this state of affairs, they were quickly disillusioned. Of course matters were not helped by the fact that I was barred from going 'down the village', where they would have had no control over the company I kept.

Thus it was that one afternoon two little boys knocked timidly at the door of The Grove. They were given cups of tea which they sipped cautiously, looking warily at each other and occasionally glancing furtively at what they must have considered the lavish furnishings of the living room. Then, under the watchful eyes of my mother and grandmother, the three of us were ushered into the spacious back yard 'to play'.

My father had recently embarked upon one of those money-making hobbies that evoked such pitiless scorn from my mother. The last one had been bee-keeping, and I have dim but terrifying memories of him periodically donning a kind of visor with flaps to protect himself against the angrily buzzing creatures while he collected their honey. This time, he had decided that great profit lay in growing mushrooms. The first phase in the implementation of this scheme consisted in the importation of innumerable bales of straw which were now 'cluttering up' (my mother's phrase) the garage, leaving our motor car exposed to the elements in the back yard.

Eventually this straw would be transferred to the loft, where it was somehow transformed into mulch from which, in what seemed like the twinkling of an eye, mushrooms of remarkable size sprouted in unanticipated profusion. Soon we were eating them with every meal, and before long this pleasure became something of an ordeal. Eventually we were delivering surplus mushrooms to every restaurant on the island. Once the first crop had been mercifully exhausted, my mother exercised her veto and the project was quietly abandoned. Such was often the fate of my father's projects: too much rather than too little success was their downfall.

For the moment the garage was filled with bales of sweet-smelling straw, which provided an ideal environment in which a child nostalgic for the womb could lose himself. Here I brought my two awkward playmates, and proceeded to improvise a succession of variations on the hide-and-seek principle. These involved elaborate rules for preventing my guests from finding me once I had tucked myself out of sight. Unfortunately, neither my prospective friends nor my mother and grandmother thought much of these artificial stratagems. Having observed the joyless goings-on for as long as she could endure it, my mother ordered me to emerge from the straw and try in future not to be so bossy. The two sniggering lads were sent on their way, doubtless the richer for a few pence or some biscuits, and I returned to my solitude, sensing a measure of disgrace in the absence of subsequent comment on the afternoon's events.

ک   ک   ک

I have drifted away from the little school down the rhododendron-fringed lane, and must now return there to confront the issue that, of all others, could make this a misery memoir: bullying.

For decades I lived with the conviction that I had been bullied unremittingly from the moment that P.J. and Blondie sidled away from their responsibility to defend me. Further, I have internalised the certainty that this bullying was a defining

factor in my personal growth, eventually leading to my sporadic activism on behalf of the downtrodden.

However, hours of reminiscence have failed to dredge up
more than one or two cases of actual bullying, and these insufficiently brutal to mark me in a way that would have brought
the matter to my parents' attention. Alongside these specific
incidents, however, must be placed the constant fear of their
recurrence, and the sense of mingled injustice and shame at
being singled out in this way by lads to whom I had done no
harm (and whose fathers, if I had thought about it, were probably collecting unemployment benefit from my father). It was
futile for me to attempt to ingratiate myself with these bullies,
as any such effort seemed itself to be regarded as an affront at
worst and a joke at best.

The field behind the school was fringed by furze bushes,
known as whins. For a time it became customary to punish
those captured in games of hide-and-seek by throwing them
bodily into these thorny plants, a penalty dubbed 'th'electhric
chair'. The invention of this punishment encouraged my mali-
cious inclusion in games from which I might otherwise have
been excluded. Furthermore, it soon became clear to me that it
would be unwise to be too ingenious in escaping detection. On
several occasions when my unfriendly mates seemed on the
verge of giving up the search for me, I diplomatically coughed
or sneezed, thus alerting them to my whereabouts while satisfying both their competitive vanity and their desire to humiliate me.

My first experience of being picked up by three or four hefty
louts and flung into the whins was agonising, but not so much
as my tormentors believed. I shouted and moaned and sobbed
and laughed in order to give the impression that I was suffering greatly while simultaneously taking the whole ordeal in

a good spirit. When nobody was looking, I practised throwing myself into the thorns, my sleeves pulled over my wrists, my socks dragged up to my knees, and eventually found that by tensing myself I could undergo the experience without too much agony. As a result, my mates rapidly tired of the game and left me alone.

The ugliest incident came from the most unexpected source, and featured the threat of physical violence without its realisation. S.D. came from the neighbouring village of Cashel, and was a good-looking, popular lad, proficient both in class and on the football field. His parents were slightly better off than those of most of our schoolmates, and perhaps for this reason I wrongly deduced that he was reasonably well-disposed towards me.

On one occasion he accompanied me along the main road after school, having some business or other to transact in Bunacurry on his parents' behalf. Although the two villages were less than a mile apart, they cultivated the self-image of irreconcilable rivals and boys from one village rarely ventured into the other (I suspect the girls were less bothered by such absurdities). I was disproportionately proud and delighted to be singled out as this interloper's companion, and lost no time in inviting him to pay a brief visit to The Grove.

Like the curator of a Great House, I showed S. into the sitting room and pointed out the piano which had become so important to me. Then I led him ceremoniously into the dining room, where tea had been prepared by the maid. I displayed the Christmas presents I had received the previous month, with as *pièce de résistance* the *Beezer Annual* which I prized less for its content than for the fact that my beloved father had given it to me. S.D. absorbed everything with a polite smile – he had been well brought up – and when he took his leave

I wallowed in the conviction that I had cemented a valuable friendship and a useful alliance.

Next day it soon became clear that all was not as I had hoped. Before class started I noticed S.D. whispering to some of his accomplices while looking derisively in my direction, and judged by their laughter that I was in for trouble. Sure enough, during the 11.00 a.m. playtime break the roughs cornered me behind the schoolhouse and taunted me for having 'wan room to *sit* in and another wan to *dine* in...' While this taunting continued, accompanied by pushes and shoves but not by blows that might have come to the teachers' attention, S.D. hovered nonchalantly in the background. This non-participation was merely tactical, however, as the miscreant approached me after school and warned me that if I didn't bring him the *Beezer Annual* next day he'd 'fight' me, a euphemism for beating me black and blue.

'Will you give it back to me?' I asked shyly, already conceding the main point.

'I might and I mightn't,' was the reply, delivered in a tone and with a facial expression that conveyed no realistic doubt as to which option he favoured.

Next day, sheepishly, forlornly, I handed over the treasured volume, never to see it again. My grief was caused less by its loss than by an obscure sense that I had somehow betrayed my father – there was a kind of pity for him mixed in with and exacerbating my self-pity. I racked my brain for a plausible lie to explain the tome's disappearance, yet never found one. It would be clearly impossible to tell my father that I had given it away in a gesture of improbable generosity, as such cavalier treatment of a treasured gift would surely have been deeply hurtful to him, or so it seemed to me. Anyway, I was an incompetent liar. The truth, however, would have brought unknown and unpredictable consequences in its wake, leading to my being permanently branded a sneak, one of the lowest forms of juvenile life, meriting the chant of *'tell-tale tattler, buy a penny rattler!'* every time I ventured into the society of my pitiless peers.

Much to my relief, no questions were ever asked about the missing *Annual*.

Why did I not stand up for myself? I have a sense that I did so on a number of occasions, but only one of these has lingered in my memory, perhaps because it was also the one and only occasion on which I accepted my schoolmates' invitation to accompany them along the route that led homewards through the fields, in defiance of my parents' prohibition.

It turned out that the sole motive for this invitation was to set up a fight between myself and a small, ferret-like boy who seemed to nurse a particularly strong dislike for me. Cornered, I put up my fists and laid into the fellow for whom, if the truth be told, I also felt considerable loathing. In no time at all he was on the ground, but instead of pursuing my advantage by continuing to pummel him, I stood back and let him get to his feet. Some treacherous blackguard now pushed me so that I staggered towards my opponent, who lashed out and punched me in the face while the rest of the gang cheered enthusiastically. Blinded by sudden tears, more shocked than physically hurt, I fled and was not pursued.

I was quick on my feet and stronger than I looked, but dreaded that forceful attempts at self-defence might bring down collective retribution on my head – for I was one and they were many! At least my two brothers, a decade earlier, had reinforced one another to some degree. While violence was a medium through which my schoolfellows moved easily and naturally, I hated it. Fleeing rather than fighting brought down on me a reputation as a coward, one in which I partly and shamefacedly concurred.

Experts agree that repeated bullying during childhood can lead eventually to stress-related illness and even to suicide. In later life I often invoked this to explain my behavioural difficulties. I am no longer convinced that I was indeed abused by my peers quite so frequently or brutally as all that: I may well have manufactured non-specific memories of bullying precisely because of the exoneration they seemed to provide.

However, I was a middle-class boy in the midst of children most of whom came from impoverished families, and I was habitually meek and shy in manner. I must not go to the opposite extreme and deny either that I was bullied or that this bullying and fear of its repetition were formative experiences. Bullying is a monstrous abuse of human rights, whether transacted between individuals, social classes or states.

That its link to my subsequent activism is no mere sublimation is proven, I think, by a strong subjective factor: that overpowering sensation of constriction in throat and stomach – of helplessness, resentment and outrage occasioned by injustice – is the same whether the powers are rogue states or aggressive louts.

By the time I had graduated to 'the big lads' in the classroom next door, Brother Angelo had retired in favour of Brother B., a much younger man the bridge of whose nose displayed an outcrop of fuzzy hair that predictably earned him the nickname 'Beardnose'.

I liked B., a kindly man who obviously had to force himself into the occasional role of disciplinarian so patently relished by his predecessor. Noticing that I was solitary in my habits, he made no attempt to coerce me into joining my schoolfellows on the football field, but engaged me in conversation as I munched my jam sandwiches in the front doorway of the little schoolhouse. In the course of one such chat, presumably in the winter of 1962, he asked me if I believed in Santa Claus. I did, but pretended otherwise, indulging in a fatal desire to show off my non-existent maturity and urbanity. His reply, detailing the history of the evolution of the Santa myth in Renaissance Europe, showed much respect for my intelligence but little insight into the infantile psyche.

He had an exquisite, melancholy tenor voice that turned singing-practice into a genuinely pleasurable experience, at least for me. There was an innocence about him that invited and facilitated mockery, but that also led to one of the most embarrassing incidents of my final year in Bunacurry Boys' School.

There was to be an evening of amateur theatricals in Bunacurry Hall, and Brother B. had decided that the boys under his charge should participate in the event. He chose the one-act comedy *Cough Water* by J. Bernard MacCarthy (1888-1979), a once-prominent playwright, novelist, short-story writer and poet from Cork. *Cough Water* (1922) is described as 'a farce in one act' and is clearly designed exclusively for the amateur circuit.

My role was that of Doctor Cronin, Temporary Medical Officer at Begbawn Dispensary. Although the doctor heads the cast list, the meatiest role by far was that of my assistant, Mike Doran, played with genuine verve by John Kilbane, a slightly older middle-class lad from Cashel. An unintentional highlight of the performance was provided by one Michael M. in the off-stage travesty role of Katty. Michael/Katty responded to every summons with a loud cry of 'Phwaat's the thrubbul?!' that, growing ever more stentorian as the evening progressed, was each time met with proportionately increasing laughter from the packed house.

Katty is described by Mike Doran as 'the girl who comes in to cook for me while the wife's away'. This strikes me as the first of a number of mildly louche elements in the scenario that must have raised my mother's eyebrows. Indeed, the only line that I could remember (inaccurately, as it happens) after almost half a century was, 'Are you having a clandestine relationship with my daughter?' This stems from Mr Carey, a rich farmer, who rightly suspects Dr. Cronin of designs on his niece Eily, 'a pretty, stylishly dressed young girl of about twenty' (the line is actually, 'she's now in that room holding a clandestine meeting with that young whipper-snapper, Dr. Cronin'). When first I read through the play I recall asking my mother the meaning of 'clandestine', upon which she snatched the booklet from me to reassure herself that Brother B. was not involving her innocent son in some kind of obscene spectacle.

And indeed there are some potentially risqué moments. At one point, according to the stage directions, 'Mike draws back the screen on door and shows the doctor and Eily embracing. Owing to the position of the others they cannot see.' Shortly thereafter, 'Mike looks again. The doctor is just kissing Eily.' Mike comments: 'He's looking at her tongue.' When 'the doctor nestles his head on Eily's breast' Mike tell us that 'he's putting a big poultice on her chest now.'

I cannot recall whether any schoolgirls were co-opted to play the four female roles, but I am quite certain that I neither kissed anyone nor laid my head on her breast. I was so obsessed with not forgetting my lines that I found it best not to allow the audience to distract me, and kept my back firmly turned towards them for the duration of the play. I had never been encouraged during rehearsals to bear in mind that the onstage proceedings were in principle directed outwards towards a potentially attentive public.

Not surprisingly, my mother was mortified by this performance, for which she was less inclined to blame myself than Brother B. When it was confirmed that the evening's entertainment was to be repeated some weeks later in the far more imposing premises of Achill Sound Parochial Hall, historic scene of her first encounter with 'the detective from Dublin', she presented B. with an ultimatum: either he would accept her services as assistant director (which he no doubt correctly assumed would mean surrendering all his authority) or she would withdraw my services as star performer. The placid Beardnose seems to have displayed unexpected defiance, with the result that my theatrical career met a premature end. I have no idea who took my place, or if the performance was simply cancelled.

Chapter 5

Standing in the gateway of The Grove, you look out over Bunacurry Village and beyond to the mysterious wilds of Ballycroy, Bangor Erris and the Nephin mountain range.

Lineens, the local grocery, post office and telephone exchange, was about half a mile down the road to The Valley. At Christmas time it would decorate its large front window with tinsel and small bells and silver balls hanging from red ribbons. The display space would be filled with toys – motor cars, teddy bears, revolvers and fancy chocolate-boxes. Villagers would congregate in the cold, small children and adults alike pressing their red noses to the glass for hours.

As ever, though, there is a grimmer memory associated with this shop. At a certain point my sister, her friend Mairead and myself began to experiment with smoking. In a remote corner of the grove or in the least visited of our outhouses, we started with funnels of newspaper which we lit and through which we sucked acrid smoke before the improvised cigarettes shrivelled up and burned our fingers.

Soon we were buying packets of genuine cigarettes, a risky venture in such a locality where there could be no anonymity. The inevitable happened sooner rather than later. One evening, Mr Lineen telephoned the house and informed my parents that I had purchased a packet of 20 Players earlier that day. Were they aware of this? My parents were both smokers, so the purchase had some plausibility – although my father's brand was the more manly Sweet Afton.

Patsy and I were both in the kitchen chatting with the maid when the summons came for me to appear before a family tribunal in the dining room.

'Did you buy cigarettes today?' asked my mother, while my father and grandmother looked on impassively.

'Yes, I did,' I replied, deciding wisely but, alas, temporarily, that honesty was the best policy.

'Why did you buy cigarettes?'

'Somebody stopped in a car outside the gate and gave me the money to go down to Lineens and buy them cigarettes.'

'What "somebody"?'

'I don't know. They were tourists.'

'And why didn't they go to Lineens themselves to buy the cigarettes?'

'They ... I ... I don't know!' (Tears were beginning to flow.)

'Admit it – you bought them for yourself. Have you been smoking?'

'Yeeees ...'

Before long the whole story had been dragged from me, and I had been compelled to implicate Patsy and Mairead, whose parents were subsequently informed of her participation in this infamy. Patsy was summoned from the kitchen and forced to watch while I was punished – 'not for smoking, which is bad enough, but for telling lies!' My father drew back my sleeves and slapped me repeatedly, as hard as he could (or would), on the palms of my hands. At first Nana was a jeering spectator – 'trying to be grown up before your time, you little liar' – but before long she was pleading with him to stop, 'that's enough now – he's learnt his lesson...'

In truth the punishment wasn't particularly painful, but it was deeply humiliating. My father was an authentic illustration that the cynical old catchphrase 'it hurts me more than it hurts you' can occasionally be true. He appeared to be on the verge of tears for the rest of the evening, and an expression more mournful than severe didn't leave his face for several days. Of course I was angry with the shopkeeper for having betrayed us, while my two female accomplices were angry with me for betraying them, but my predominant feeling was one of regret for having hurt my father's feelings. When reconciliation came – 'we'll say no more about it' – I could have kissed his large hands abjectly, but probably just buried my nose sheepishly in my book.

ς   ς   ς

Further down the Valley Road, a turn to the right leads into the forbidden regions of Bunacurry Village proper, and a little further on looms the Catholic Church, with a handsome presbytery opposite (where once a madman cornered the curate in his kitchen).

Every second Saturday I went to Confession. This entailed taking my place in a queue which was seated along the bench nearest to the Confessional, a kind of booth in the centre of which the priest sat, sheltered from the waiting penitents by a full-length curtain, and from the penitents on either side of him by a sliding screen covering a narrow-mesh grill that very inadequately disguised their identity from him.

Apart from the incident of the mythical tourists who had commissioned me to buy cigarettes, I never had much of significance to tell the confessor. Telling lies, being disobedient, using bad language and being inattentive at Mass were my standard sins; I varied the number of times I had supposedly committed each of them and the order in which I trotted them out so as not to betray the fact that I was merely repeating a formula. The penance never consisted of more than a few Hail Marys and an Act of Contrition ('Oh my God, I am heartily sorry for having offended thee...'), probably supplemented in the case of the cigarettes by an entire decade of the rosary.

Nonetheless, I found confession a profoundly disagreeable experience, feelings that were augmented when I read a biography of Padre Pio, the stigmatic Italian priest who would be canonised by Pope John Paul II in 2002. Apart from being periodically beaten by devils, appearing in two places at once (known as 'bilocation', which I confused with 'biliousness', a condition I imagine he wasn't spared), generating a flowery perfume known as the 'odour of sanctity', and of course regularly bleeding from wounds corresponding to those of Christ on the cross, this versatile holy man had second sight and could read people's minds at a great distance. He was in the habit of bellowing from the confessional at certain unfortunate penitents kneeling outside that they should go home, and not return until they truly repented of their sins. None of the Bunacurry priests gave the impression of excessive sanctity and none showed evidence of stigmata (I looked at their hands to make sure), but I still nervously anticipated the moment when a harsh voice would issue from behind the curtain condemning me to endless mortification because of my hypocrisy.

I invariably attended Benediction of the Blessed Sacrament on Saturday evenings and Mass on Sunday mornings with my father. We always chose the same place to sit, which memory convinced me was under the Station representing 'the scourging at the pillar'. However, there is no such station, and memory has been up to its tricks again.

In order to alleviate the boredom of these sacred ceremonies I would have recourse to my Missal, which contained a number of short prayers the recitation of which entailed remission of venial sins for periods of up to 300 years. Totting up thousands and tens of thousands of years of indulgences was an attention-devouring occupation that also had the benefit of passing time in an apparently pious and legitimate manner, with the ultimate benefit of reducing the duration of Purgatorial torment.

Mind you, one of my teachers had told me that Purgatory would consist in suffering the worst thing you could possibly imagine for a period the length of which you could not even begin to imagine, so I sometimes felt that these indulgences were merely a drop in the ocean. The possibility that I might avoid Purgatory altogether by being in a state of perfect grace at the moment of my death never seemed very plausible to me, as I considered myself to be hopelessly wicked, even if in a relatively minor ('venial') way.

The alternative, Hell, was a real presence in my life. It was essentially the same as Purgatory, but it never ceased, because, having died in a state of Mortal Sin, you could never be purged. In some confused way I was convinced that the principal cause of Mortal Sin and hence eternal damnation was sex, although the word had not yet entered my vocabulary. Later on, when I lost all belief in God, Satan hung around for a long time, perhaps to admire his handiwork.

Past the Church the road winds to the left. A right turn leads to The Valley and eventually brings us to the seaside at Dooniver. This was one of my father's favoured fishing spots, and we would also occasionally swim there, although the beach was stony and hurt my feet. I reflected that this wouldn't be a problem were my mother to allow me to go barefoot on a daily basis like so many of the village children, whose feet I believed were entirely immune to pain. Perhaps her refusal to allow this even in fine weather was inspired as much by class consciousness as by concern for my welfare.

The road from Dooniver winds through Dugort, which nestles picturesquely beneath the bulk of Slievemore, then swivels left to Dookinella where it again meets the main road to Keel. Opposite the imposing Achill Head Hotel, there once stood the Achill Head Cinema, and it was here, aged six or seven, that I saw my first film.

My parents must have felt that *The Wizard of Oz* was a foolproof choice from every point of view, including, of course, the 'moral' one that was ever uppermost in my mother's mind. However, they reckoned without the perverse psyche of their last-born.

I was, to begin with, alienated by the size of the hall, the presence of so many chattering, chewing and smoking strangers, and the loud music blaring from loudspeakers high in the walls. Once the lights dimmed and the curtains mysteriously parted, I was terrified out of my wits by the spectacle of an aeroplane rushing towards me from the screen, and sought to cower beneath the seat in front much to the disgust of my family and the amusement of neighbouring spectators.

As far as the feature film was concerned, I was at a disadvantage in that I could understand very little of what was being said. This problem would persist down the years, and was partly caused by defective sound systems and partly by unfamiliar accents. My bewilderment rapidly turned to horror as the talking scarecrow appeared, to be followed by the even more macabre tin man. Unable to figure out the connections between events, and unable to follow the dialogue, I saw *The Wizard of Oz* as a confusing succession of terrifying images. The benign elements – even the little dog Toto – seemed to pass me by completely, and the happy ending did nothing to assuage my sense of having witnessed some dark and threatening mystery.

In adult life I have watched *The Wizard* several times with great pleasure, and have never been able to reconnect with this initial reaction.

Chapter 6

It was a foregone conclusion that, like my siblings before me, I would learn piano. After all, there was an instrument in the house and it would have offended my mother's fastidious sense of economy to have 'let it go to waste'.

She herself was our first teacher. Her entire musical experience consisted in having played double-bass in the school orchestra of the St. Louis Convent, Kiltimagh, where she underwent her secondary schooling. I, who must have been five or six years old when I qualified for her stern instruction, was excited at the prospect of being able to decipher the musical hieroglyphs that so fascinated me and that enabled Patsy to produce such mellifluous sounds. I was in no doubt that learning to read the notes enabled one automatically to play the instrument, as if reading and playing were magically connected.

I was, therefore, doubly shocked and disappointed to find that there was an entirely separate and parallel process of manual training to be endured before I could render the simplest melody. The resultant disillusion had traumatic force and led to a total loss of enthusiasm for the project of piano-learning, to which I was subsequently held by coercion and threats.

Daily practice was rigidly enforced between 7.00 and 7.30 p.m. For a year or two these sessions were supervised by my mother, whose presence in the sitting room at least alleviated my fear of being alone at night, particularly during the long winter months. Nevertheless, I was eventually trusted to practise on my own, casting fearful glances behind me as I stumbled through my repertoire.

When my sister was eight years old she was subject to this same regime. One evening, she was disturbed by a noise behind her and turned around to behold, in her own words, 'a dishevelled grey-haired man who had managed to get one leg in the window but was unable to heave himself inside'.

'He was mumbling away to himself, taking no notice of me. I could easily have run out the door, but I suppose I was stunned, paralysed with fear. Luckily, Mom, who happened to pass by the door of the sitting room, decided to check why I wasn't practising. I didn't even turn to look at her when she came in the door; my eyes were riveted on [the intruder]. She couldn't see him because of the window alcove.

"What is it?" she asked.

"A man," said I.

So Mom grabbed the first object within reach – a vase – and started hacking away at him.

"Ah, take it aisy, Ma'am, take it aisy," said he. By that time I'd recovered my senses and made a dash for the door.'

The interloper was a certain Doctor H. who had been disbarred from medical practice when the isolation of a more remote island had driven him to drink. He was notorious for entering people's houses when in his cups and in need of a few hours shut-eye. It was not unknown for respectable people to be disturbed at their breakfast by the sound of the good doctor descending the staircase, having commandeered a bedroom for the night unknown to his involuntary hosts. According to my father, he would walk in the normal way if he had been drinking stout, but walk backwards if his tipple had been whiskey. I heard two versions of his death: he either fell down the stairs (at home) or was strangled by his own tie. I only hope he didn't hang himself.

On this particular occasion he had apparently driven his car into the ditch and had wisely decided to postpone doing anything constructive about it. Seeing an open window he had steered himself towards it, forwards or backwards as the case may be, but his plans were brutally frustrated by our vase-wielding mother.

I must have been five years old at the time and was kept in the dark about this event, although Patricia claims that nothing else was talked about in the household for days. I think I was a very self-absorbed and inattentive youngster. By the time I had reached piano-playing age I was acquainted with the story, and eventually added it to the growing store of terrors that made practice a fearsome experience.

Nonetheless, I acquired the rudiments and was packed off to take weekly lessons at the convent school in Achill Sound, five miles from Bunacurry, and site of the Labour Exchange of which my father was now manager. As was usual at the time, he worked half a day on Saturdays; accordingly, my lessons were scheduled for Saturday morning. I was delivered to the school door an hour early, and was obliged to sit quietly in the front of the classroom during the teaching sessions that preceded my own.

The teacher, Sister de Pazzi, would often present me with an apple from the convent's orchard to help me while away the time. I came to dread this well-intentioned ritual, as the apples were speckled yellowish things, soft of texture and mouldy of taste. She would wait for me to bite into this offering with a tactful simulation of appreciation before she turned to her pupil of the moment; hence I was unable to secrete the thing in my bag with a view to disposing of it afterwards.

Although Irish and not Italian, Sister de Pazzi, whose name we pronounced to rhyme with 'jazzy', was named after a Renaissance Florentine saint who, according to a Catholic encyclopedia, was allowed by God 'to be tried by terrible inward desolation and temptations, and by external diabolic attacks...' Did my teacher wish to emulate her namesake's 'ardent love of suffering that made her genuinely wish to live long in order to suffer with Christ' by teaching piano to little children in the far west of Ireland? While she had limited patience with my predecessors on those long Saturday mornings, occasionally resorting to the application of ruler to knuckles, she was gentleness itself with me. This testified either to my comparative diligence or to the social status of my parents.

I have no memory of Sister de Pazzi's face, although I can well recall the hushed, almost caressing tones in which she addressed me. The skin of her slim, conspicuously veined hands was of a waxen pallor that fascinated and slightly repelled me. It was impossible to imagine that she had any sort of life outside of the Saturday classroom, that she had hair beneath her headdress, or legs beneath her immaculate black habit. She guided me through the first few grades of the Royal Irish Academy of Music syllabus, then floated out of my life as I imagined her floating from that classroom into some mystical, candle-lit space of her own for six days of every week.

The lesson over, I would stroll as far as Brett's newsagent to wait for my father to pick me up after work. Here I would install myself beside the revolving magazine rack and browse to my heart's content. I was indulged in this habit because my father and Mr Brett were old friends and fishing companions.

The shop is still there, but has expanded into a miniature supermarket that evokes nothing of its earlier aura.

'Comics' were what my father brought home from Bretts for myself and my sister every day of the week: for me *Beano*, *Beezer*, *Wizard*, *Hotspur* and *Eagle*; for Patsy, *Judy* and *Bunty*. While Patsy disdained to look at my comics I would devour hers, often memorising the dialogue, so *posh* and distinct from our domestic dialect.

These were quite different productions from those aimed at little boys. The adventures of Dan Dare or Cripple Dick Archer, the crude biffing and bashing of boyish story-lines contrasted sharply with the more realistic distress of one of the 'Four Marys' that the ends of her hair turned up instead of curling. Even so, I thought the illustration of her was very fetching, and wondered uneasily if such a thought was sinful.

Eventually I reached sufficient technical proficiency to gain enjoyment from playing the piano, and no longer had to be coerced into evening practice: I would race for the piano as soon as I returned from school. However, I cannot claim to have been drawn to music by some precocious affinity with the classics. Indeed it was trash like that notorious salon warhorse *The Maiden's Prayer,* by T. Badarzewska, a piece once described as a 'dowdy product of ineptitude', or Leander Fischer's *The Robin's Return* that infected me with a longing to outdo my sister's facility in the execution of trills, arpeggios and consecutive octaves. A matter of sibling rivalry, then, rather than aesthetic aspiration.

Was I aware, aged nine, that these trifles were inferior to the music of Mozart and Beethoven that I was obliged to learn for my examinations? I don't think the question entered my head. These pieces followed a very similar pattern, and made an excellent impression on visitors who were ushered into the sitting room for a display of childish pyrotechnics. The arpeggios and passage-work that were stereotyped features of such music could be pulled off with a measure of shameless bluff and ingenious pedaling. Alas, I then transferred this trickery to music that required more advanced technical capabilities. The combination of natural facility with laziness and impatience, together with the absence of a rigorous teacher in later life, impeded my becoming a truly accomplished pianist – although this was my second-highest ambition after that of becoming the world's greatest composer.

This decision was made when I was ten years old, by which time my sister had started playing pop songs 'by ear'. I greatly envied this skill, and resented the fact that I did not seem to possess it. What I could do was improvise successions of makeshift tunes and harmonies that struck me as every bit as good as those reproduced by Patsy. On one occasion, determined to impress somebody, I played one of these confections for our maid Theresa, successor to the much-lamented Ann, telling her it was a hit song I had just heard on the radio.

'Well, what do you think?' I asked, as soon as I had finished.

'It's all right,' she said, hesitantly enough to suggest that she meant something different.

'Only all right?'

'Well, I don't think that it's something you heard on the radio. I think you made it up yourself. It's all right.' And she left the room to resume her duties.

I interpreted these ambiguous words as a negative critique, and decided that the world's greatest composer was not going to attempt writing pop songs.

ک   ک   ک

Meanwhile, there was that green- and cream-coloured Dansette gramophone.

Only my father was permitted to remove this precious object from the cabinet beneath the bookcase, place it carefully on a small table near the fireplace, and plug it in. My elder siblings were permitted to operate it and did so in an insouciant manner, whereas once I acquired the skill and responsibility necessary for this delicate task I never performed it without a sense of awe mingled with anxiety.

Most of the records in our small but disparate collection were scratchy 78s, many without a cover, and most consisting of performances by 'Count' John McCormack (Pope Pius XI had made him a Papal Count). My mother's devotion to this Irish superstar was boundless, the quality of his voice being enhanced by the stolidity of his nationalism and Catholic piety.

There were, however, several more up-to-date records. I have no idea how *Smoke Gets in Your Eyes* by The Platters found its way into our home – presumably one or other of my brothers was responsible – but it rapidly became a favourite of mine. I wanted to look like the all-American Pat Boone, whose photograph graced the cover of an LP of his songs that included the Everly Brothers' composition *Gee But It's Lonely*:

> *Got dad's car and chauffeur*
> *but that's no good to half a pair*
> *Gee but it's lonely bein' alone;*
> *might as well go home...*

Reading this now it seems obviously tongue-in-cheek, yet for many years this song ran through my mind whenever I found myself in the gloomy circumstances it evokes (minus car or chauffeur, of course).

Our collection also contained classical records, all vocal, which were the property of my father. There was a Gigli album including the Bach-Gounod *Ave Maria* with soupy female chorus, harp and strings. There was an album of extracts from Gounod's *Faust,* Nicolai Gedda in the title role, and a photograph on the cover of Boris Christoff looking suitably demonic and horny (in the literal sense) as Mephistopheles. Gedda cropped up on another album about which I remember nothing except that it included *Dies Bildnis ist bezaubernd schön* from Mozart's *The Magic Flute* and the *Flower Song* from Bizet's *Carmen.*

While I loved the former, I believe that the latter was the key listening experience of my childhood. The sinuous, 'oriental' tune on cor anglais, the trembling violins and repeated plucked notes on low strings, the ecstatic main melody, the unaccompanied scale leading to Gedda's almost unimaginably beautiful high B, and perhaps above all those impossible harmonies with which Bizet delays his final cadence – every one of these details sent a shiver down my spine. I surmise that these latter harmonies may have smoothed my path, later on, towards appreciating the disconnections of 'atonal' modernism.

I recognised in some inchoate way that while Frank Ifield's yodelling and Pat Boone's crooning (and, later on, Elvis, the Beatles, Freddie and the Dreamers, Manfred Mann and the rest) were fine in their way, nothing could compare to the frisson induced by Don José's lamenting love song from his prison cell. Perhaps, after all, this was the kind of music that would repay a lifetime's loyalty.

Chapter 7

As 1962 became 1963 I was the only Deane sibling still living in The Grove.

Declan, as eldest son, had been groomed for the priesthood from an early age, a destiny to which he was fully and indeed enthusiastically reconciled. He was now resident in the Jesuit novitiate in Emo House, a stately Gandon-designed neoclassical mansion surrounded by opulent parklands in County Laois. Jackie (John) had followed his example, and was installed in the Holy Ghost Fathers' seminary in Kilshane, County Tipperary. I recall family visits to both these imposing and rather intimidating establishments, meals taken at huge mahogany tables under massive chandeliers, walks in carefully tended gardens, and a general sense of awe that, nonetheless, for me never translated itself into a 'vocation'.

Patsy had been sent to the Loreto nuns' boarding school in St. Stephen's Green, Dublin. She returned to Achill for the 1962 Christmas holidays a changed person, full of anecdotes about the lives of sophisticated city girls, not unlike my imaginings of those 'posh' young ladies in *Judy* and *Bunty*.

It was decided to move the remainder of the family to Dublin. I had already been taken two or three times on short visits to that city, and had boasted to P.J. and Blondie that Nelson's Pillar – a forty-metre high doric column in the centre of O'Connell Street, destroyed in 1966 by a bomb planted by the IRA – was so high that airplanes had to fly around it. The thought of moving to Dublin thrilled me, and I can recall not a twinge of regret at leaving my familiar haunts.

Neither can I recall any particular apprehension at the prospect of a new life, a new school, perhaps a new onslaught of bullying. Did I imagine that city boys were a different species, far too concerned with negotiating their complicated city lives to interfere with such a harmless little person as myself?

ڪ   ڪ   ڪ

When I embarked on these childhood reminiscences, I firmly believed that I was about to tell a tale of woe that would explain many of the difficulties that attended my later life. The challenge, it seemed to me, would have been to avoid writing a 'misery memoir'. In the event, as I concentrated on certain key memories and sought in vain for others, I discovered that there had been precious little misery. I further concluded that my later conviction to the contrary had been a fabrication calculated to provide an excuse for my life's eventual descent into darkness and chaos.

This does not mean that I now reinterpret my first decade as some kind of idyll, dominated by sweetness and light. My own peculiarities, my shyness, morbid fearfulness and sometimes comical hypochondria precluded this. But I was cherished by my parents, my needs were attended to, and my embryonic talents were nurtured. Furthermore, I did not always experience my solitariness as a burden; I enjoyed wandering the fields, climbing trees, sitting in the window seat gazing at Ballycroy, reading or drawing. I came to love playing the piano and toying with the possibility of composition. And anyway, I became less solitary as the years passed, hanging out with a variety of companions who were not exactly friends, perhaps, but whose company I enjoyed for short periods and who seemed willing to forgive me my class origin.

In many respects, after all, I was a 'normal' little boy: I enjoyed kicking a football around, whether on my own, with my father, or with select companions, although not in any kind of team, where the bugbear of *responsibility* might raise its unwelcome snout. While I preferred Gaelic football – which allowed the ball to be handled – I also loved soccer. I considered myself to be a fan of Tottenham Hotspur and Jimmy Greaves, of Manchester United and Bobby Charlton. I was obsessed with guns and swords, cowboys, Indians, and feudal knights and their suits of armour. I knew all the ranks of the British and American armies, from private to field marshal. I despised little girls of my own age, and was simultaneously fascinated by them.

'Cherished by my parents' – undoubtedly. But those two people had markedly different ways of displaying affection. My father's was openhearted, and free from the reserve that often characterised his public persona. He could be playful and mischievous, and while he brooked no misbehaviour, he never seemed entirely at ease with his role as 'the boss', as my mother designated him with a certain undertone of irony.

She was the true disciplinarian of the household, but as a matter of social and familial convention deferred to 'the boss' when punishment became physical, as in the sorry case of our experiment with cigarettes. Unfortunately for Patsy, this did not apply in Bunacurry Girls' School, where our mother apparently felt that she was obliged to display lack of favouritism towards her daughter by regularly 'making an example' of her.

I know now that there was a measure of bitterness and disappointment blended in her uncompromising posture towards the world. By all accounts she had been a lively young woman, fond of dancing and socialising, and on her deathbed I would have a ghostly glimpse of this other, airier persona. If iron had entered into her soul there must have been a serious reason. It is not unlikely that this was the discovery that those who had warned her against marrying Donald Deane had had a point: that he was an alcoholic, and that although he loved her dearly there were times when – as with all sufferers from his condition – he loved Dame Ethyl Alcohol more.

When I was in my late teens and my father had disappeared on one of his occasional drinking-bouts, my mother opened her heart to me about the hardships she had endured throughout her marriage, on top of having borne four children and suffered two miscarriages. It appears that in the course of their wedding reception my father, who had been drinking freely, disappeared. At last, sick with foreboding, she had herself left the party and driven around until she found him asleep in a ditch.

One could hardly imagine a marriage getting off to a less auspicious start. In now confiding this terrible story in me was she openly and uncharacteristically seeking to enlist my sympathies, which had always, and in her eyes unjustly, leaned towards my hopelessly endearing father?

This was an ineffably sad situation. My mother was surely a loving person, but had difficulties expressing any strong feelings other than indignation. My father elicited affection effortlessly, just by being himself. Children are cruel and egotistical, and judge the respective virtues of their parents mainly according to the degree of fondness demonstratively bestowed upon themselves.

Unfortunately, these unreflecting evaluations linger into adulthood, particularly when the adult in question (myself) hasn't really grown up. My mother's heartbreaking tale had its momentary effect, but soon my father returned from his drunken wanderings, broken and contrite, and was subjected to the kind of harangue that tended to alienate sympathies that had briefly shifted in her direction. Before long he had recovered, she had relapsed into reticence, and once again her thoughtless youngest son had ceased to be an ally.

Many years ago I heard that at some point during those Achill years my parents had split up, and been reunited by a priest. In my own more melancholy days I convinced myself that my conception was a result of this clerical gentleman's interference, and I frequently cursed him when in my cups or suffering their aftermath.

On another occasion, my father had crashed the family car – presumably when under the influence – and his passenger had consequently lost an eye. This was an old friend and colleague who lost no time, justifiably of course, in suing him. As a result, for many years an appreciable portion of his salary was deducted in order to pay the substantial fine that had been imposed. This must have led to no little hardship in the Deane household. Was this the immediate cause of my parents' temporary separation?

I should add that my father, in all other respects, was a man of fanatical probity. Repeatedly, as manager of the local Labour Exchange, he was in receipt of 'directives' from the Social Welfare Minister of the day that he should reverse this or that decision about payment or non-payment to this or that constituent. Repeatedly he had refused to submit to these directives, and as a consequence had been subjected to threats from on high, as well as to the withholding of a well-merited promotion.

It is hardly surprising that he began to despise his job, and sought alternative employment that would have enabled him to make use of his linguistic skills (he was literate if not fluent in French, German and Russian, and fluent in Irish). Success in making this change in his life would have had the added benefit of justifying, in the sceptical eyes of his wife, the amount of time that he spent reading all those books and magazines he acquired in the post.

But he never succeeded, and it would appear that his drinking played a role here too. There were occasions when he went away to Dublin or Belfast to take this or that exam but took to the bottle as well, thus letting the opportunity slip away, a little further each time.

Throughout my Achill years I had not the slightest inkling of his addiction. I can recall only one occasion when he unexpectedly returned from work early in the afternoon, talking in an uncharacteristically incoherent manner, swaying perceptibly, and giving off an unfamiliar and indefinably discomfiting aroma. Having put him to bed, my mother assured me that he had fallen ill and been given some very strong medicine by the doctor in Achill Sound, that it was nothing serious, and that he would soon be better.

I have little doubt that in earlier years he indulged himself with greater frequency than this. Were there occasions that, in my blithe self-absorption, naivety and credulity, I either misinterpreted or somehow ignored? Was there a menace hovering over us throughout that first decade of my life of which I was quite simply unaware?

I must leave this possibility open. When my mother lay on her deathbed, I witnessed an utterly different person from the woman I thought I had known for over thirty years. I believe now that I never really knew her at all, and feel that mixture of regret and guilt that, generation after generation, is the lot of countless sons and daughters.

Part Two

The imagination of a boy is healthy, and the mature imagination of a man is healthy; but there is a space of life between, in which the soul is in a ferment, the character undecided, the way of life uncertain, the ambition thick-sighted: thence proceeds mawkishness.

– John Keats (Preface to *Endymion*)

Chapter 8

In the summer of 1963 my mother and I travelled to Dublin together. Of course this rupture did not coincide with the end of my childhood, which had several years still to run. Within the new urban environment, however, it acquired an entirely different tempo and aura.

Although on the face of it The Grove was an attractive property, it had still not been sold by the time my mother and I left, so this must have been a period of intense anxiety for my parents, something to which, as usual, I was impervious. My mother must also have worried greatly as to whether Dad would hit the bottle in her absence, but presumably solemn promises were exacted, and the fact that Nana was in his care dampened any inclination he might have had to kick over the traces.

At first we stayed with my cousin John Cassidy, Jerry's twin brother, and his wife Breda in their home in the north Dublin suburb of Beaumont. Although our hosts were kind, I was very uneasy in their home – I have never been a good guest. My mother and I had little to say to each other, and words often led to misunderstanding and tension. After a few days she took me aside and harangued me about 'contradicting' her in front of other people; even if she was in the wrong, which she sarcastically admitted 'was often the case' (she did a very distinctive line in sarcasm), it was not my place to embarrass her in front of our relatives.

My meagre appetite, never hearty, struck Breda as both worrying and perverse. In front of my mother, who seemed rather amused, she lectured me sternly about picking at my meat while always being able to wolf down a dessert. I was constantly reminded of the existence of starving children in Biafra, whose plight never struck me as having any particular bearing on my own, and whom as a consequence I was privately inclined to wish to the devil.

Cousin John did everything in his power to keep me amused while my mother set about furnishing our new house, including attempting to teach me the ancient Irish game of hurling, for which my father was also an enthusiast. Like everything else that was voluntary but that I could not master at once, I abandoned it as soon as I could convince John that he was wasting his valuable time.

John owned a guitar and encouraged me to teach myself to play it with the help of a manual. Finding that the chord of E minor was readily accessible, I assumed that further progress would be equally speedy. When this turned out not to be the case, and that joining chords together to make musical sense was even more difficult than learning to play them in the first place, I rapidly lost interest in the instrument. From both these abortive ventures, John must have drawn his own pessimistic conclusions about my diligence and application. However, he refrained from reproaching me.

Griffith Avenue is a lengthy thoroughfare stretching from Marino to Glasnevin via Drumcondra. It was here, between the junctions with Calderwood Road and Grace Park Road, that my parents bought a house boasting the name Sunningdale.

This was proclaimed by a small sign hanging above the porch, but although we left this in place we never used the name.

Of course the house was considerably smaller than The Grove. It yielded few opportunities for exploration and concealment, there was no lake, and its front and back gardens were far more modest than the six wild acres I had hitherto taken for granted. But that was fine! The fact that we were now in the big, exciting city compensated for the wide open spaces of my receding infancy.

Naturally I missed our grove, the plane trees that lined Griffith Avenue offering no real substitute. Beautiful and lofty as they were, they had been shorn of all lower branches so that climbing them was not a realistic option. My sole attempt to access one via the front garden fence merely led to my clothes being stained with mossy green, and a scolding from my long-suffering mother.

During that summer of 1963 we were joined by Theresa, who had been so little impressed by my tentative first musical composition, and who would stay for a few months before vanishing definitively from my life. In her company I was allowed to explore the city centre, an experience that was a delight for me but must have been purgatorial for her. I rapidly developed a penchant for darting across busy streets between honking cars, pushing my way through the densest crowds, waiting superciliously for her to catch up, then rushing away again. This must have been unspeakably aggravating for her, yet she never scolded me nor complained to my mother. Had she done either, Mother would probably have taken her side and soundly scolded and perhaps even punished me, but poor Theresa could hardly have been confident of this.

Before long I was using my pocket money to take extended journeys on my own, boarding the first bus that came and travelling to its terminus. Here, I would stroll around for a while to no particular purpose before returning. Dublin in 1963 was a city so placid that such excursions were deemed safe by even such a controlling parent as my mother. Soon I had acquired a familiarity with the city's geography far surpassing my acquaintance with the nooks and crannies of Achill Island, where my adventures were curtailed by fear of escaped lunatics. It never occurred to me that such unfortunates were even more likely to be loose on the streets of the capital, where the presence of so many other people seemed reassuring.

As summer wore on I found that I pined for my father and my piano in equal measure. The former was remediable by his occasional weekend visits. The latter admitted of more regular if short-lived remedy in the shape of Waltons Music Store in North Frederick Street. Here I would sometimes spend ninepence on a loose-leaved Lilac Edition of such popular classics as Beethoven's *Für Elise*, or Schubert's *Marche Militaire*. I would try these out on one of the display pianos if the shop was empty of customers. That the staff would allow me to do this without protest is as remarkable as the fact that I so far overcame my painful self-consciousness as to risk their interference, and testifies to the degree that piano playing had already become a kind of addiction.

ﺵ   ﺵ   ﺵ

Sunningdale had cost my parents some £17,000. Given that The Grove was eventually sold for less than a quarter of that sum, the move to Dublin must have entailed considerable financial loss, particularly since my father was obliged, once he joined us, to take a demotion from his managerial rank. My mother, too, would no longer be principal but merely an ordinary teacher in Stanhope Street Girls' Primary School.

In September 1963 I was enrolled in St. Mary's Primary School, Marino, run by the Christian Brothers. The litany of demotions to which the Deanes were being subjected continued apace, as it was decided that instead of starting sixth class I should repeat fifth. The standards of Bunacurry Boys' School could not match those of St. Mary's. In particular, my knowledge of Irish was judged inadequate to the requirement of studying every subject – including English – through the medium of 'the first official language of the state'. Things could, indeed, have been even more demoralising: at first I was to be consigned to class 5B, practically among the dunces. However, it appeared that this class was already overcrowded, so I was transferred willy-nilly into the A stream and warned that I would have to be extra diligent.

Of course, I was prepared for the worst: 'up from the country', friendless, inept at Irish, I was a natural candidate for bullying, and it was obvious from the start that the class – larger than the entire population of Bunacurry School – included quite a few rough diamonds. Nonetheless, the worst never happened. The most negative response I experienced was a kind of condescending curiosity, and most of the boys, once they found to their probable disappointment that I did not have a particularly 'funny' accent, rapidly took me more or less for granted.

Indeed, the only person who mocked me for my origins was Brother T., himself from remote County Donegal, who scornfully referred to me as 'our culchie'. He was a bit of a glamour-puss, with blond wavy hair and a dashing, smug manner, and was generally disliked. When he introduced us to algebra, I initially took to it with such enthusiasm that on one occasion, when I was the only boy to get everything right in the set homework, he publicly accused me of having cheated.

Perhaps taken aback by the tearfulness with which I denied this, Brother T. let the matter drop. After class, a certain Cagney approached me. This lad, not without physical resemblance to his Hollywood namesake James 'Top o' the world, Maw' Cagney, was top of the class and had a sardonic manner. I was wary of him because, for no reason that he troubled to explain, he had decided that I was 'a bit of a spiv', a description that would have delighted me in my teddy boy phase, but now merely mystified and slightly offended me. Naturally, I assumed that he would capitalise on my discomfiture and repeat Brother T.'s accusation, but instead he said: 'That was rotten – you're obviously just real good at algebra. Brother T. is a louser', upon which he swaggered off. Although the enigmatic Cagney never bestowed any amiable attentions on me subsequently, I was overwhelmed by the throwaway kindness of his remark. This softens the memory of an otherwise disagreeable event.

From that day on, I lost interest in algebra.

The Christian Brothers have enjoyed two kinds of bad reputation. The first was for physical brutality. The second, resulting from many cases of child abuse at home and abroad, was either unknown at the time or – more likely – not spoken about. I had no experience of either form of abuse from a Brother during my year at St. Mary's. Still, there was a kind of emotional violence behind Brother T.'s determination to mock and humiliate me at every juncture, and I never forgave him for it.

Physical violence, on the other hand, was the province of our other teacher, who was a layman. Mornings were evidently a bad time for Mr K., and hence for any of his young charges who proved troublesome before the lunch break. His favourite trick was to ask you a question and stand beside you as you fumbled for an answer. If you took too long about it, or gave an incorrect answer, he would suddenly bring the heels of his hands against both your ears, leaving you stunned and temporarily deafened. This was surely a dangerous and possibly illegal procedure, even in those days of unconditional consent (in Ireland, at any rate) to corporal punishment.

Each morning began with a Gaelic spelling test, typical of the stratagems with which our educational establishment set about alienating the Irish from their native language. Ten words were read out; if a boy misspelt five or more he was obliged to bring his copybook home to be signed by a parent. On one of several occasions when this befell me, Mr K. examined my copybook attentively then told me to stand up.

'Deane!' (First names were taboo.)

'Ye-es, Sir.' (Standing awkwardly, and blushing uncontrollably.)

'Who signed this?'

'My mother, Sir.'

'I don't think she did.'

'Sir?'

'It doesn't look like her handwriting. I think you forged this.'

'No, Sir, I didn't. My mother signed it.'

'I don't think so. Sit down.'

I sat down, trembling and terrified, but there were no further consequences that day. Clearly Mr K. decided that the infliction of humiliation and anxiety sufficed to punish me for a misdemeanour which he may or may not have believed I had actually committed.

That evening I told my mother what had happened, and was taken aback by the cold fury of her reaction. Without a word, she seized her writing pad and rapidly wrote a note which she let me read. In words dripping with sarcasm she apologised for her unpractised scrawl – she had, after all, only been a teacher for thirty years or so – however, in future she suggested that he should consult her directly rather than publicly shaming her son with a false accusation.

Next morning, tremulously, I handed Mr K. this incendiary document and sat down. He opened it slowly, briefly fixing me with his bloodshot glare, and read it with features that became increasingly flushed. At last he slapped it down on his table and sat motionlessly gazing into space for a few moments, during which the silence in the room seemed to throb.

'Deane – stand up!'

'Ye-es, Sir.'

'Did I accuse you of lying?'

This is the moment when the hero of a British boys' adventure story would demonstrate the incipient stiffness of his upper lip and respond, heartily, 'Yes by George, you did, Sah!' Unfortunately, although such an accusation had indeed been forthcoming before some thirty witnesses, I was no hero and crumpled at once.

'No, Sir.'

There was a further silence, during which he looked with unmitigated disgust at my mother's document, but not at me.

'Be careful with your accusations in future.'

And that was the end of it. Furthermore, although nothing had been resolved, it was the end of my persecution by Mr K., who chose henceforth to treat me as if I did not exist. From that moment on, although both teachers were clearly my enemies, their aggression was entirely passive.

For a time it appeared as though my favourite sport, Gaelic football, was going to offer me an opportunity to distinguish myself. After a few trials, it was decided that I was good enough to be on a school team, a distinction that made me proud but intensely nervous. Our trainer was the harsh-voiced Brother O., who would have been one of my teachers had I remained in the B stream. While I had expressed a desire to be goalkeeper, this responsible position was already reserved for the biggest boy in the class. Instead, I was to be a fullback, a defender second only in importance to the goalie.

The first game in which I participated was also my last, and I cannot recall whether it was against a team from another school or from within St. Mary's itself. If I had had any illusions about winning being less important than the cultivation of sporting virtues, they were rapidly shattered. Repeatedly, as an attacker advanced with the ball into my quarter of the field, Brother O. urged me in the most savage tones to 'bring him down! *bring him down!!*' Repeatedly, unwilling as I was to break the rules by blatantly tripping my opponent, I allowed attackers to bypass me and confront the goalie. At last, fed up of this, the latter urged Brother O. to 'take him off, he's no good!', to which the Brother eventually agreed, thus ending my inglorious career as a Gaelic footballer.

Meanwhile, my father paid a flying visit in order to deposit Nana and the piano. As it happened, on the night of his arrival I was supposed to participate alongside a number of my schoolmates in a competitive event in the Mansion House, residence of the Lord Mayor of Dublin. This involved the choral speaking of Gaelic poetry, in which lines of verse were passed from one group of boys to another according to inexplicable laws having no apparent connection to the content of the text (which I possibly did not understand anyway).

I was miserable that I was obliged to be absent for the one evening when my father was in Dublin, and when he took me on his knee and ran his large hand over my hair, I dissolved in tears. It was my mother, with her characteristic and under-appreciated mixture of kindness and rigour, who made the decision that I was to stay at home. She telephoned the school and brusquely conveyed the message that I would not be participating.

Of course this in no way endeared me to the Brothers, and the fact that our choir came away empty-handed from the competition was laid at least partly at my door. Still, there were no long-term negative consequences from this. Is it conceivable that someone in authority was humane enough to understand that, under the circumstances, I was not to be blamed for choosing my father before the school?

And yet this memory fills me with guilty unease. Retrospectively I see the willingness of my parents to exempt me from responsibility as having helped convince me that I could simply renege on participating in any transaction that was uncomfortable for me, even if I had solemnly committed myself to it.

On balance, my year with the Christian Brothers was neither particularly unpleasant nor unhappy. The boys did not bully me, or harp on my outsider status, and some half-hearted friendships were developed. The teachers were more obnoxious than otherwise, but lost interest in me at an early stage. I had to work hard to catch up academically, and was proud of the fact that although my results put me somewhere in the bottom half of the class, I successfully avoided relegation to the dreaded B stream. Still, my Gaelic never reached the level of fluency that was taken for granted among my classmates, so history lessons went over my head and geography fared little better. My parents, perhaps influenced by the ugly incident of the forgery accusation, decided that I should move on.

Chapter 9

The piano was installed in the ground floor room we duly dubbed 'the piano room'. I borrowed every volume of piano music from every public library in North Dublin city. To each of these handsome buildings, built with funds from Dale Carnegie, I cycled on a red and white bicycle that my parents must have given me as a present, and that I took so utterly for granted that I have no recollection of their doing so.

I borrowed Beethoven's thirty-two *Piano Sonatas*. I borrowed the works of Schubert, Schumann, Brahms and Chopin. But, above all, I borrowed Liszt's *Hungarian Rhapsodies* which fascinated me endlessly; I think that already I recognised their inferiority of inspiration to the abovementioned masterpieces, but this didn't matter – they were wild and wonderful, and full of *cadenzas* the visual effect of which (rising and falling swarms of tiny notes!) attracted me as much as the pleasure of mercilessly butchering them.

I ploughed through everything, never pausing to iron out difficult passages, bluffing shamelessly when necessary. It must have been torture for anyone in the next room, and perhaps in the next house, but while I was sometimes asked if there were no quiet passages in any of my favourite music, no attempt was made to curb my enthusiasm.

Eventually, it was decided that I needed further tuition. My mother accompanied me to what was then called the Municipal School of Music in Chatham Row, off Grafton Street in the city centre (subsequently a branch of the DIT Conservatory). I was introduced to Finn O'Lochlainn, a tall, sallow-complexioned man in his fifties, who I would later decide resembled the Hungarian composer Bela Bartok.

At first this patient, soft spoken and good-natured gentleman struck fear into my easily frightened heart. I played a couple of short pieces for him, and sight-read something or other, upon which he asked me some questions which I answered with monosyllables or not at all. Several painful silences punctuated the interview, invariably broken by my mother's impatient injunction to 'say something!' which in turn led to Mr O'Lochlainn's reassurances that these were *very hard questions*.

Although I emerged from this interview on the verge of tears and with heavy clouds hanging between my mother and me, in reality it went rather well. It didn't take long for me to overcome my shyness towards Mr O'Lochlainn. He was a tolerant and, if the harsh truth be told, a rather lazy teacher. I had a natural talent, a slightly unnerving skill at sight-reading, and an aversion to practising scales and technical exercises. The teacher's and pupil's skills and deficiencies complemented each other only too satisfactorily. On the debit side, technical failings that might have been corrected became ingrained; on the credit side, Mr O'Lochlainn's willingness to discuss music with me as with an equal led me to feel more and more at ease within the classical realm and enhanced my self-respect.

More demoralising were my experiences in the theory class taught by Miss P., a brisk, middle-aged lady with greyish-blue hair. I had never heard of 'theory' and much of what went on in the class mystified me completely, in particular the rhythmic exercises that entailed mouthing permutations and combinations of four repellent syllables: *TA-fa-TE-fe, TA-fa-te TE-fe-te,* etc. The requirement to beat out time-signatures like a conductor was entirely new to me, but not to my classmates. I had no conception of the difference between an up- and a down-beat, and when asked to beat 4/4 time flailed my right arm around helplessly while my peers giggled and I blushed ignominiously. Miss P.'s response was to shake her head and cluck her tongue in disgust, but not to demonstrate the correct procedure.

On the other hand, I was proficient at ear-tests, well able to repeat short melodies and to identify the notes of a chord once the bottom note was named.

Above all, I excelled in answering questions about the set work, Prokofiev's *Peter and the Wolf*. Although I had never heard it before and, unlike the others, did not possess a recording or a score, I was able to identify the different orchestral instruments without difficulty. These tell-tale signs of musicianship somehow escaped Miss P. who, a few years later, on being told that I had won an award in the *Feis Ceoil* (an annual competitive music festival), conveyed her astonishment with the words, 'I never thought that fella had a note of music in his head!'

When Mr O'Lochlainn asked me how I was progressing at theory, I told him bluntly that I was getting on badly, that I hated it and that it was a waste of time. 'Leave it with me,' was his encouraging response. Sure enough, a few days later he telephoned to say that I need worry no more – he had secured me an exemption from the hated classes.

Had I endured Miss P.'s insensitivity for a year or two, I might actually have soaked up some of the theory that I was eventually obliged to learn for myself. Had I then mastered the reasonably straightforward art of beating time I might later have progressed to conducting, a skill the lack of which probably didn't help my future career. In taking the more comfortable route and bypassing these disagreeable lessons, I was aided and abetted by a well-meaning adult who may thereby have unwittingly done me more harm than good.

ک   ک   ک

Only temporarily discouraged by Theresa's lack of enthusiasm for my Achill improvisation, I resumed composing as soon as the piano was in place. However, I had not overcome the suspicion that there was something a little shameful, a little *sissyish* (in those days there were few more derogatory adjectives if you were a proud little boy) about the very idea of composing classical music. But the bug had seized me, and the manuscript book I had bought for my abandoned theory classes was crying out to be filled. I began to write piece after piece in the style of whichever composer I had just been playing, rarely finishing one before starting impulsively on the next.

On the wall behind the piano hung a central heating radiator so constructed that I could cram sheets of wholly (or, more often, partly) filled music paper between its two constituent metal plates. This became the receptacle for a succession of unfinished works reaching all the way to Op. 11, No. 4.

Soon, inevitably, winter arrived, the heating was turned on, and it became necessary to dispose of the evidence. What was to become of this cache of mazurkas, nocturnes, sonatinas, fantasias and rhapsodies in the styles of Chopin, Mozart, Beethoven and Liszt? I could perhaps have concealed them beneath the growing piles of sheet music atop the piano, but my sister or mother might have unearthed them, in which case I felt certain that I would be subjected to intolerable ridicule.

Alas, there is an anticlimax here, as I have no idea how I solved the conundrum. One way or another, the products of my first period disappeared from the face of the earth.

Patsy was now a day pupil at Loreto College. Music was one of her subjects, and as a result I was obliged to yield the piano to her for an hour or two daily. I didn't resent this, as I enjoyed listening to her practise pieces by Kabalevsky and Poulenc that helped ease me into the harmonic world of twentieth century music. Among the books that she borrowed from the Loreto school library was Edward Lockspeiser's *Debussy*, which I practically memorised, playing its short musical examples over and over again and speculating as to how they might continue. Surely I was not the first enthusiast to be spurred to composition in this way?

During the summer of 1964 it was decided that I should continue my education in Belvedere College, a venerable Jesuit institution in Great Denmark Street, around the corner from Walton's Music Shop. Since I had missed the official entry examination, a special private test was set up for my benefit, my brother Declan's status as a Jesuit-in-the-making having presumably made this possible.

I was placed at a table in the study of the Junior School's Prefect of Studies – Jesuitical for headmaster – Fr. Murphy. He was a tall, fair-haired, bespectacled man of scholarly and somewhat ironical demeanour, elderly in my eyes, but probably in late middle age. Despite my morbid timidity, I took an immediate liking to him and was to retain it throughout my Belvedere years – and beyond, for I would sometimes meet him at concerts later on. He handed me a succession of papers, in I recall not how many subjects, each of which he corrected as I completed the subsequent one. As a result, he was able to inform me that very afternoon that I had been successful – clearly the Christian Brothers had done their job well.

This was not all, however. Father Murphy there and then offered me the job of organist at the Benediction service that took place daily at midday, and at which the entire school would be present, seniors as well as juniors. Since I was clearly intimidated at this prospect, particularly as I had never played an organ before, he brought me to the chapel and allowed me to improvise for a few minutes at the simple old instrument, with the further inducement that I could practise on it whenever I wished. Not alone was I now a Belvederian, but I was the college organist! There was undoubtedly an element of snobbery mixed in the justified pride with which I announced these two pieces of news to my parents, and they were suitably impressed.

ﺱ   ﺱ   ﺱ

Later that summer our posh English relatives descended upon Dublin. They rented a white bungalow on the coast road at Dollymount, but spent much of their time with us in Griffith Avenue.

I thought that my new urban status might have automatically brought a certain urbanity in its wake, but if it had, it had not yet developed sufficiently to overcome the shyness these exotic people inspired in me.

My cousin Aileen had inherited more of her mother's Frenchness (which I still mistook for Arabness) than any of her siblings, but while Madeleine was exuberant and florid in her gestures and conversation, Aileen seemed restrained, withheld, contained. She gave me no encouragement, was barely civil towards me, yet on occasion I fancied that in some intangible way she acknowledged me as her contemporary at least. Simultaneously, I suspected that even this recognition existed only in my imagination, and I was probably right. I am not sure whether my father would have dubbed my proto-adolescent attachment 'calf love' had he known of it, but for me it was an occasion of vast confusion, pain and delight – in other words, something fully equal to any adult passion.

One evening everyone except the two youngest children went to the Gate Theatre to see what they thought was a stage adaptation of James Joyce's *Dubliners*. I imagine that my mother must have been in two minds about this excursion, given that for her the name Joyce was synonymous with 'dirt and filth' – her shorthand for anything remotely relating to sex – so I deduce that Uncle Jack, the raffish war hero, had talked her into it.

At some point during the evening Aileen and I started play-ing hide and seek in what was hardly a propitious environment for such a game, the Griffith Avenue house signally lacking the nooks and crannies of The Grove. Soon the game became more boisterous, and I found myself chasing her from room to room, and eventually, unfortunately, catching her.

My fair cousin drew back and administered a sharp slap across my cheek.

Had I been too rough with her? Or had I been too gentle? Had I, in fact, impulsively and inappropriately sought to snatch a kiss? Or was she merely being capricious and displaying her capacity to do as she pleased?

Shocked, hurt, humiliated, I fled to the sitting room and, locking myself in, switched on the radio. Although most of the important details of this domestic drama have vanished from memory, I can recall the irrelevant fact that Brian Boydell's orchestral piece *In Memoriam Mahatma Gandhi* was being played, a piece whose elegiac character chimed with my desolate mood.

Of course I fantasised that Aileen would try to gain access to the room and, finding it locked, would tap on the door, perhaps entreating my forgiveness. This unlikely narrative was nipped in the bud when the two families returned prematurely: it turned out that the *Dubliners* in question were not James Joyce's Ignatius Gallagher or Gabriel Conroy but the bawdy, rowdy, beardy folk group featuring Ronnie Drew and Barney McKenna.

A few days later 'The Jacks' flew home, and I never saw Aileen again. She died eight years later in London, where she was seeking to make it as a folk singer. That momentous and mysterious slap is the only intimate secret that we shared; I certainly mentioned it to nobody, and she probably forgot it immediately. Almost half a century later, it still smarts.

Chapter 10

The Christian Brothers had indeed done their work well, and many of the gaps in my education had been filled. As a result, I found that Belvedere's Junior School was a comparatively relaxing experience.

Undoubtedly, as I have hinted, part of the appeal of Belvo (as it was known) was snobbish: donning the green cap and black blazer with the college crest yielded an unmistakably *arriviste* gratification. It was exhilarating to cycle to school and back through the still relatively tranquil streets of my adoptive city, innocently and egotistically convinced that motorists and pedestrians alike were observing me and declaring admiringly, 'there goes a Belvederian!'

Teaching was now entirely through English, there was little threat of corporal punishment, and there was far less homework to distract me from my preferred pursuits – music, reading and television.

Being the school organist lent me a welcome degree of status as well as affording me half an hour's respite from class: the Benediction ceremony for which I played (following in the footsteps of my mother) was confined to Senior School students. This respite, therefore, lapsed the following year when I in turn entered Senior School.

In the end-of-year examination I came second in my class. This, alas, was the acme of my Belvederian academic career; it was all downhill from there.

Once I had made the transition to Senior School, it was expected that I would participate in Belvedere's sporting life, a Great Tradition deliberately evocative of the English public school. Gaelic football and hurling, of course, were excluded as too redolent of native sweat; soccer, too, was frowned upon, no doubt because in England it was deemed the province of a lower class of person, even if that negative distinction hardly applied in Ireland. This left cricket and rugby.

These strongly contrasting activities were total mysteries to me, yet I was expected to engage in them without their veils being lifted. I endured two utterly baffling and boring games of cricket during which I stood around, chatted to my mates and twiddled my thumbs for an eternity before being summoned on to the field for a few minutes of perplexing activity, which I performed to nobody's satisfaction.

My rugby career lasted all of half an hour, my single bout of possession of that absurdly shaped ball terminating abruptly and brutally when I was ground into the wet mud by a classmate whom I had always regarded as nerdish and puny.

Thus ended, for all time, my participation in sport.

The College liked to boast of its distinguished past pupils, most notably the violinist Hugh Maguire and the multi-millionaire businessman (and, just as importantly for the Jesuits, former rugby star) Tony O'Reilly. Less often mentioned, if at all, was James Joyce, the College's most celebrated alumnus but a figure of dubious repute in Catholic Ireland. Joyce attended Belvedere between 1893 and 1898, and was exempt from fees thanks to his father's profligacy.

As in Chapter 4 of Joyce's *Portrait of the Artist as a Young Man*, I was one day summoned to the office of one of the senior Jesuits and asked the same question that was posed to Stephen Daedalus: 'Have you ever felt that you had a vocation?'

The priest in question was very pleasant and unintimidating, so I was prepared to be completely honest.

'I thought so for a while, Father, when I was young.'

'When you were young, eh? So long ago?'

'Yes, Father. Particularly because both my brothers went for the priesthood. But now I think I want to be ... some kind of musician.'

'Well, a musician, of course. That's very nice. And it can also be a way of serving God.'

'Of course, Father.'

And that was all. Of Stephen, Joyce wrote: 'How often had he seen himself as a priest wielding calmly and humbly the awful power of which angels and saints stood in reverence!' While still living in Achill I too had occasionally seen myself in that light, but there was nothing particularly pious about such a vision. In general my prayers were rather mechanical and even mercenary – the calculus of indulgences, the assiduous performance of penance in order to forestall the agonies of Purgatory or Hell – while my attendance at church was characterised by boredom and distraction, with little or no sense of spirituality. I had no doubts, not then, about the existence of God and the ineluctable truth of all dogmas of the Holy Roman and Apostolic Church, but they scarcely impinged on my inner life. I was never going to follow in the footsteps of my brothers, and the kindly Jesuit clearly perceived that there was no point in urging me further.

A less benign Joycean aspect of Belvo was represented by the Senior School Prefect of Studies Father G., known to all and sundry as Jacko, and a very different proposition to Father Murphy. This holy man must have read *Portrait of the Artist* and modelled himself admiringly on that novel's hellfire-breathing Father Arnall. Although Jacko was most noted for the ferocious relish with which he fulfilled his duties as administrator of corporal punishment, I was rarely subjected to this particular medicine. In fact, 'lines' and detention were the preferred means of discipline in the College. Once more, my family link to a prospective Jesuit, rather than exemplary behaviour on my part, may well have played a part in the leniency of my treatment.

However, Jacko had other forms of terrorism at his disposal. He would randomly select a class and enter quietly, without knocking, upon which the boys would rise to their feet with alacrity and profound unease. Amidst a deathly hush, Jacko would survey the assembled ranks with a look of deep disdain, a chalky substance on his lips suggesting that he had been foaming at the mouth not long beforehand.

'Sit!' he would snap, and like a pack of hangdog curs we would obey.

I don't know if Jacko had any pets among the boys – I doubt it greatly – but he most certainly had pet hates. Two boys – E.K. and P.E. – inspired him to particular heights of malevolence, being excoriated by him repeatedly as 'men-about-town'.

'E.K. – stand up!'

Contriving to slouch even in performing this action, E.K. stands up.

'Are you a *man-about-town*, boy?'

'Em, no Father.'

'Repeat after me: '*my friend has money, but I do not have any*'.

'My friend has money, but I don't have any, Father.'

'I sincerely hope you do not have 'Annie', boy – Annie is *a shopgirl!'*

'Sorry, Father?'

'ANNIE IS A SHOPGIRL!!'

This explosion echoes shockingly through the room, the school, and possibly the universe. E.K.'s normally pasty face has turned vermilion. Jacko, as pleased as any successful stand-up comedian with the effect he is producing, now modulates his voice to a quieter but even more menacing timbre.

'The word I am looking for is pronounced 'enny', boy. Repeat it after me...'

'Enny, Father.'

'But I have heard that you have been seen in the company of – *shopgirls.*'

'Me? No, never, Father.'

'I should hope so, E.K. Let me NEVER learn that you – or your fellow *man-about-town* P.E. – have been seen in the company of – *shopgirls*. Belvedere boys' – and he pauses dramatically to let his cold, somewhat rheumy eyes travel over the unprepossessing specimens of natural superiority cowering before him – 'Belvedere boys *do not keep company with SHOPGIRLS!'*

'No, Father.'

Jacko would depart as suddenly as he had arrived, with a scowl at the boys and a dignified nod to whichever embarrassed teacher had seen his class so flagrantly disrupted.

E.K. also lived in Griffith Avenue. I regarded him not just as a friend of sorts but also as a role model, if one that I could never realistically hope to emulate. He modelled himself on Ilya Kuyakin, the suave and enigmatic turncoat Russian spy in *The Man from U.N.C.L.E*, an American TV series then being aired by the BBC. Ilya was blond-fringed (so was E.K.) and filled his sleek polo neck sweaters very elegantly (E.K. attempted the same, with somewhat less elegance).

Although by now our single channel had been supplemented by three British stations, my viewing was strictly policed and *U.N.C.L.E* was implacably out of bounds. As a result, I relied on E.K.'s lurid accounts of the saucy goings-on between Ilya and a variety of young women who were invariably, it seemed, as naked as made no difference.

Then there were those legendary parties that E.K. and his sidekick P.E. claimed to have been regularly attending, at which *girls* (although possibly not *shopgirls*) were present, and who, it was darkly hinted, were prepared to *do things*, the nature of which – amid exchanged nudges and winks – was left to my sadly ill-furnished imagination.

Given that I had not been invited to any of these possibly mythical parties, and none were planned for the foreseeable future, I formed the daring plan of taking the initiative and or-ganising one myself. This idea, when proposed to E.K., did not elicit the enthusiasm I had hoped for. Nonetheless, knowing that my parents would be out late on one particular evening, I foolhardily asked my mother if I could invite some friends around, who would bring some of their friends in turn, and whom I guaranteed to have off the premises by my official bed-time of 10.00 p.m.

'Would any of those friends of friends be girls, by any chance?' asked my mother, her eyebrows raised and her lips pursed in a characteristic mixture of incredulity and amuse-ment, with a hint of imminent irritation.

'Well, yes, I think so...'

'Forget it,' was the unambiguous response, while my father merely looked on compassionately, but with a certain air of drollery. Abashed but possibly also a little relieved, I regret-fully announced the bad news when next I met E.K. and P.E.

'Probably just as well,' said E.K., nodding significantly to his accomplice, in whose languid company he was always mark-edly less friendly towards me.

'Why?'

'Oh, it wouldn't have been a very good party anyway,' chimed in P.E.

'Why not?' I persisted masochistically, instinctively antici-pating a bombshell.

'Because you're not sexy!' concluded the treacherous E.K., and the two chuckling men-about-town strolled off about their louche business, leaving me to contemplate my devastation.

ﺱ   ﺱ   ﺱ

Around this time, for want of reliable two-legged friends, I de-veloped the habit of bringing home dogs that would latch on to me as I returned from school or the shops. The last straw was when one of these, an amiably snuffling boxer called Rocky (for these were not anonymous strays, but belonged to neighbours whom I had never met), deposited from his quivering rear end a wriggling worm on to the sitting room carpet.

Accordingly, I was forbidden from consorting with pro-miscuous neighbourhood pets; but, in compensation, I was to have a dog all of my own! Having cast around for some time, my parents at last located a six-month-old Alsatian pup in the West Dublin suburb of Crumlin, where he lived amidst a size-able brood of boisterous children and cheery pups.

The dog, not entirely pedigree but for all that the most beau-tiful canine creature I had ever beheld, was friendly but wary. He accompanied us with considerable reluctance, and in the car he whimpered and panted and drooled. Once we got him home he retired into a corner and lay there in a state of disconsolate inertia sharply contrasting with his prior playfulness.

The Crumlin family had named him Rebel, after the German Shepherd in a TV series called *The Adventures of Champion*. He apparently interpreted his name as implying passive resistance to all attempts to cheer him up. Only when out walking would he display any animation, inspired not by me but by Griffith Avenue's myriad plane trees and their standing invitations to sniff and urinate.

I yearned for Rebel to be reconciled to me as his master and friend, but when he showed no such inclination, my parents gave me a stern ultimatum: 'one more week, and if he doesn't cheer up we'll have to bring him back to Crumlin – sometimes you have to be cruel to be kind!'

On the verge of despair, I tried everything. I would lie beside him on the floor tickling his stomach, repeating 'Rebel, Rebel, good dog, good fella!' over and over again, but his tail might wag once, politely, before subsiding into immobility. I mewed like a cat in his ear, but he merely eyed me suspiciously without lifting his head from the floor. I tried to run with him along the avenue, but he would stop dead, dig his heels in, and force me to haul on the lead until it was obviously hurting him. Then I would desist and we would stare at each other dismally, with something like mutual hostility, until I yielded and let him choose his own pace homewards.

And then, towards the end of that fatal week, everything changed. Rebel was lying on the front lawn, seemingly oblivious to the world around him. I picked up a twig and idly poked him with it, then threw it away more in weary disgust than in anticipation of a reaction. But Rebel leapt to his feet and ran after the thing. Picking it up in his teeth, he crouched expectantly, a look of unmistakable mischief in his large eyes.

I feigned to pounce on him, and he scampered off to the opposite end of the garden where he crouched again, chewing on the twig and, oh victory supreme, *wagging his tail.*

That evening I was able to replicate this experiment for my parents, who duly lifted the threat of returning him to his former home. Rebel was mine! And yet, in a deeper sense, he was not mine and never would be. Abandoning passive resistance, he took up active disappearance, absenting himself from home for several hours at a time, returning shamefacedly but none the worse for wear just when we had given him up for lost, or worse (of course Laddy, his ill-fated predecessor, was not far from my memory).

At this point my father took things in hand. Henceforth it was he who fed the dog, washed, brushed and combed him, let him out last thing at night, and at weekends took him for much longer and more energetic walks than was my slothful habit. He also began to teach him tricks, a process Rebel seemed to enjoy: sitting down, giving the paw, lying down, fetching his plate, walking to heel. Rebel responded immediately to these determined attentions, and before long had clearly renounced his vagabond ways once and for all. In return, he adored my father, and since I adored him too I could not hold it against the brute. But of course, I *did* hold it against him: he was *my dog,* yet would have forsaken me and Griffith Avenue without a backward glance. Clearly, then, he thought of himself as my father's dog, and thus was a traitor.

ﺱ   ﺱ   ﺱ

In October 1965 my grandmother died aged 91. My brother Jackie, who had entered the novitiate of the Holy Ghost Fathers rather than follow Declan into the more rigorous clutches of the Jesuits, had for some time been convinced that he had no vocation for the priesthood. Nonetheless, he had been reluctant to abandon this course while Nana was still alive, so ecstatically proud was she of her two clerical grandsons. He now called it a day and moved in with the rest of us in Griffith Avenue while pursuing a BA degree in English literature at University College Dublin.

I found him rather surly and apt to snap at me, but on the other hand I was delighted to browse through the books that he brought with him, ranging from the poetry of T.S. Eliot and Gerard Manley Hopkins to a copy of the Douai Bible that I was eventually allowed to appropriate, and that I scoured for the texts of Handel-like oratorios that would never be composed.

That same year, a kind neighbour brought me to the Gaiety Theatre to attend my first symphony concert. The RESO played a programme that included Hindemith's colourful *Metamorphoses on Themes by Carl Maria von Weber*, which I loved, and *Two Pieces for String Orchestra* by the Irish composer John Kinsella who, my escort and I concluded unanimously, must have been mentally deranged.

Although by now I was playing and listening to such composers as Debussy and even Stravinsky, the best I could come up with when requested by Patsy – who was now learning the clarinet – to write a piece for her to play at Loreto College's 'Pupils' Concert' in May 1966, alongside Bach's *That Sheep May Safely Graze*, was a *Mazurka in D Minor* that was both conventional and inept. There may be some excuse for the conventionality – perhaps I felt that the audience would expect it – but having already reached Op. 11, No. 4 in an earlier life, there was no excuse for the ineptitude.

Nonetheless, this was my debut as a composer, before a sizeable captive audience of pupils and parents. Patsy's accompanist was one Deirdre McNulty, at the time a well-known

Dal's wife!

concert pianist. More interestingly, the junior and senior orchestra were conducted in works by Dvorak, Purcell, Mascagni, Schubert and A.J. Potter by none other than Colman Pearce, B.Mus, who in later years would conduct the premieres of a number of my works as well as the first CD devoted entirely to my music.

I took my bow from my place in the audience in such a daze of pride that I had to be forcefully pulled back into a seated position. It was official: I was a composer, alongside J.S. Bach!

Chapter 11

Slowly but surely I became addicted to the BBC Third Programme, which in 1967 became simply Radio 3, and which concentrated primarily on classical music. I noticed that there was a socket in the side of the family's transistor radio into which it was possible to insert the cable from the TV aerial, thus boosting the station's comparatively weak signal. However, since the TV set was in the living room, I could only listen when nobody else wanted to watch television. Even at that, reception was appalling, and my unfortunate family's sonic sufferings were greatly compounded.

The old Dansette gramophone had by now outlived its usefulness, and been replaced with a state-of-the-art Ferguson record player which, although a great improvement on its venerable predecessor, came without loudspeakers.

In 1963, the New Electric Theatre in Talbot Street (in the centre of the city) had been fitted out with a huge three-strip screen and renamed the Dublin Cinerama Theatre. That summer I watched *The Seven Wonders of the World* several times, seating myself as near to the front of the cinema as I could, and revelling in the sensory immersion.

I quickly associated the Cinerama experience with that of sitting before a huge orchestra. This curious megalomania began to influence my choice of gramophone records, and led me

via several of Mahler's symphonies to Schoenberg's sumptu-
ous *Gurrelieder*, of which I had read a description as the ultimate in *fin de siècle* choral and orchestral gigantism.

While this initial impetus may have been a little vulgar, I
rapidly became seduced by the richness of its late romantic
melodic and harmonic idiom. I listened to *Gurrelieder* in-
cessantly, even underlining (probably in ballpoint pen, a terrible habit) the most unctuous passages in the printed libretto
that came with the Kubelik recording I had bought in Harry
Moore's legendary record shop in Dawson Street.

Gradually, I moved on to other works by Schoenberg, until I was learning to enjoy some very uncompromising music
indeed. In the space of a few months my own compositions
had moved light years from the banalities of my *Mazurka in D
Minor*. I wrote two untitled piano pieces reflecting the fateful
influence of a new discovery, the German composer Karlheinz
Stockhausen, and submitted them to a composing competition
organised by the College of Music. The adjudicator was Joseph
Groocock, a popular teacher and broadcaster of highly conservative inclinations.

The only other entry was a *Piano Sonata* by a young man
several years my senior, written – according to Groocock – 'in
the style of the Elizabethan virginalists'. I greeted this information with a curl of the lip, convinced as I was that such archa-
ism would be dismissed without appeal. However, Groocock
decided that my opponent's pastiche of a 400-year-old model
was more efficiently constructed than mine of a living one,
and I was relegated to second place. I stalked out resentfully
without collecting my score which I had stupidly submitted in
manuscript. Perhaps it will turn up some day among the late
Professor Groocock's papers.

Also in 1967 I achieved my first distinction as a pianist, taking second place out of twenty or so competitors in the Under 14 contest at Dublin's *Feis Ceoil*. The adjudicator was an Englishman called Joseph Cooper, whose voice was familiar to me from the BBC radio quiz show *Call the Tune*. Once everyone had played the set pieces (I remember that one was by Grieg) he found himself unable to decide whether first prize should go to myself or a girl called Mary B. Consequently, a sight-reading contest took place between us which I won without difficulty.

Cooper consulted at some length with a variety of *Feis Ceoil* officials, then announced that, since he had been advised that the first prize could not be shared – his preferred option – he was obliged to award it to Mary B. despite her having botched the sight-reading. Ultimately, the set pieces were what counted, and she had displayed rather greater technical assurance in her execution of them than I had.

Naturally, I was shocked and disappointed by this – as I thought – *craven* decision. I complained to all who would listen that I had been robbed, and that Cooper had put cold technique ahead of native musicianship.

My sister, however, disconcerted me by not taking my side. Mary B. was a fellow Loreto girl, she had often heard her play, and indeed she had performed in the concert at which my *Mazurka* had been premiered. She worked hard at her technique, and such an accomplishment could not be dismissed as having no connection to musicianship.

I was incensed. What did she know about it? I would prove to them that I was a true musician, and that this was more important than being a mere technical automaton! Thus I made a matter of misguided principle out of ignoring some of the best and most well-intentioned advice I had yet received.

ک   ک   ک

Unfortunately, my musical and general educational progress were in inverse proportion. Since scaling the heady heights of second place in Junior School, subsequent examinations had seen me lapse until I reached a lamentable twenty-third place in second year. None of the Deanes had ever sunk so low! In effect, I had become a dunce in every subject but English and French, while my Irish was just barely holding up. Music was not on the syllabus, and German was an optional extra that would have entailed coming to school at 8.30 a.m. instead of 9.15.

A new school year started, to my deep discontent. Having sunk towards the bottom of the barrel, I was filled with dread that my continued slippage would take me into the second stream – that after the Christmas exams I would become what I thought of as 'a B boy'. Yet my extracurricular passion for music and, increasingly, literature robbed me of the will to hoist myself back into the ranks of class leaders.

I did score an unexpected triumph when I took first place in The Bishop's Exam, an annual test of Christian knowledge for third year students. I wrote an impressively dogmatic essay refuting Existentialism, with particular reference to Sartre and Camus, neither of whom I had ever read (except for Sartre's short story 'The Wall', which I disliked). The prize was a great disappointment: a glossy book on Egyptian archaeology, which interested me not a jot.

Otherwise, all was gloom. At each day's lunchbreak I would eat the banana sandwiches prepared by my mother, queue in the canteen for a chocolate éclair and Club Orange for dessert, then lounge idly around the yard trying to look nonchalant and inconspicuous until the bell summoned us back to class. It felt chillingly like my early experiences of embarrassed solitude in the playground of Bunacurry Boys' School, without the threat of 'th' electric chair'.

In an attempt to court popularity I engaged in all kinds of trivial mischief, usually directed against teachers with a high tolerance level. I would make animal noises without moving my lips, and use a rubber band to catapult soggy lumps of chewed paper at the backs of the heads of those boys least likely to seek revenge. These cowardly pranks would disrupt the class somewhat, annoy the teachers somewhat, and amuse my classmates somewhat, but I would still spend lunchtime on my own, feigning nonchalance and swallowing my dignity with my chocolate éclair.

But now my body intervened. Whereas my dislike of Marino had manifested itself in periodic head colds, my growing resistance to Belvedere materialised through my toes. At first, a single toenail grew into the flesh, obliging my mother to prize it out with a nail file, having first soaked the foot in scalding water. A few days later a second nail required the same treatment. To no avail: within a matter of weeks I could boast eight ingrown toenails, the maximum possible given that the little toes are apparently immune. Walking became impossible, and I was removed from school.

I was taken to a Fitzwilliam Square specialist. Dr Brown, or Browne, took one look and opined that I was the victim of a rare bacterial infection, and would require hospitalisation at the Bon Secours in Glasnevin. So it was that this new phase of my life took place under the auspices of the same Bone-Suckers who, in Tuam, had ushered me into the world.

The operation was conducted under general anaesthetic. Afterwards, my bandaged feet protected from the bedclothes by a frame, I panted all day with thirst and vomited periodically, driven to the verge of madness by the sight of a bottle of orange juice that some insensitive person had placed on the window sill. Once these after-effects had eased off, I slept like a baby.

My recovery was briefly marred by the presence in the same ward of a toothless old man whose condition, parlous on his admission, deteriorated rapidly in the days that followed. At first he was quiet during the day, but at night would engage in conversation with invisible interlocutors. One evening while my parents were visiting he suddenly began to call out for his son Justin, who had been with him that afternoon. The desperate, monotonous melancholy of this call was unnerving:

'Jaaaaw-sht'n! Jaaaaaaw-sht'n!!' (Justin.)

By now I was able to hobble slowly around the ward. I decided to show off my Good Samaritan inclinations, and shuffled over to him.

'Can I help you at all? Would you like me to call a nurse?'

Suddenly his eyes snapped open and were completely alert, and in a perfectly normal, slightly mocking voice, he put me in my place.

'Sure I wasn't talkin' to you at all, little boy!'

And then he was gone again, his eyes elsewhere, his surroundings elsewhere, and the cry of 'Jawsht'n!' again resounded through the ward.

My mother was highly amused: 'So much for your good intentions,' she observed. That night the toothless man was silent; next morning the orderlies carried his body elsewhere.

On my release from hospital, my mobility was considerably impaired and Dr Brown(e) advised me to stay out of school for another two weeks.

Simultaneously, providentially, I read an advertisement in the daily paper for an institution that prepared students for admission to university by means of correspondence tuition.

Further enquiry revealed that, in order to sit the Matriculation exam, I only needed five subjects of which English, Irish and (the only truly sour note for me) Latin were prescribed. Could I choose French and Music as my remaining subjects? Indeed I could.

With throbbing heart I laid this dramatic proposal before my parents and, to my joy and amazement, they accepted it. My father, I suspect, agreed because he sensed and sympathised with my growing discontent. My mother may well have been influenced by her single encounter with Jacko at a parents/teacher meeting, when his patronising attitude had strongly prejudiced her against Belvedere.

ڪ   ڪ   ڪ

Just a few days before Christmas that year Jackie, Patsy and I were preparing to leave the house for a performance of Handel's *Messiah* in the National Boxing Stadium, where it was at that time an annual fixture. Our mother was in a state of some anxiety, because Dad was an hour or so late in coming home from work.

And then we heard his key in the door. Rebel rushed to greet him as usual, jumping on him, whining joyously, licking the backs of his hands. But something was very amiss. He was preceded by that peculiar 'medicinal' odour that I had once sniffed in Bunacurry. His eyes were watery, his manner furtive, his bearing unsteady. As he removed his overcoat, my mother stood framed in the living room doorway, silent, livid, her arms severely folded. We took our leave, and on our way to the car I again displayed my almost unfathomable innocence.

'Dad is acting kind of funny. Is he sick?'

'He's drunk,' replied Jackie brutally, and the world cracked a little.

'Are you sure?'

'Of course I'm sure. It's not the first time, and this means it probably won't be the last. I'm afraid there'll be trouble now.'

Handel's glorious oratorio came and went, but everything was overshadowed by this awful new fact: Dad had come home drunk, and there was going to be trouble.

Chapter 12

From now on, my father's every homecoming was awaited with as much anxiety as pleasure. A ritual had evolved whereby I would wait in the front hall until I heard his key in the lock, then open the door before he had a chance to turn it. Since the *Messiah* incident this game had lost its innocence, as I dreaded encountering his intoxication yet was reluctant to discontinue the practice. On one occasion when he arrived rather the worse for wear, he commented in the strange wheedling tone that was one symptom of his alcoholic personality's emergence:

'I know you smell my breath every time I come home!'

My father was what was known in those days as a dipsomaniac, a drinker who could avoid alcohol for months or even years on end, but whose binges might then last for days. Over the next twelve months, they became more frequent.

Once, when he returned in a state of befuddlement, my mother lectured him contemptuously and mercilessly then retired to bed. He sat in his armchair gazing vacantly into space, gently stroking Rebel's head.

'Rebel doesn't hold it against me,' he murmured at last, to nobody in particular. 'Rebel is the only one who doesn't hold it against me.'

Birthplace in Tuam, County Galway

Maternal grandparents

First memory – in a Westport photography studio

With the wirrasthroo *expression*

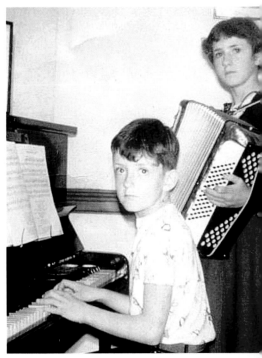

At the piano with sister Patsy, 1962

Christmas in Achill, 1962

Raymond on Mweelin, 1962

Brother Declan and cousin Jerry

Brother Declan and Uncle Jim

Bunacurry view

View of Slievemore from Bunacurry Pier

Teddy boy Raymond, with cousins Aileen and Jacqueline

As a Young Irish Composer, TCD   *Participants in 'Bayreuth' concert, 1972*

Cologne home in 1976–77 on Adolf-Fischer-Strasse

Piano recital in Oldenburg, 1985

With Dublin's Lord Mayor, Bertie Ahern, 1986

In the Canaries, November 1987

In Grogan's, 1987 or 1988

During the making of DVD 'Order and Disorder' (photo by Veronica Carroll)

'I don't hold it against you,' said my principled sister, kneeling beside the two of them, petting the back of the puzzled but ecstatic dog, thus vicariously petting our father.

I could take no more of this and retired to the bedroom that I now shared with Jackie. The fact was that I *did* hold it against him. I *did* resent the entrance into my life of a Mr Hyde so at odds with the Dr Jekyll that I loved and admired. Moreover, I resented the fact that I held these things against him, and that despite all my love and admiration I was incapable of my sister's unstinting compassion. I felt that I was somehow failing him by my inability to be fully supportive.

On another occasion, when we had eaten a dejected supper without him, he arrived home drunk and ensconced himself in the sitting room in the hope of avoiding confrontation. Mother chewed her food silently for a few moments then abruptly stormed out, her facial expression threatening war. Soon we could hear her raised voice from the sitting room, ascending more shrilly after each inaudible interjection from him.

Then there came the unmistakeable but unprecedented sound of hand against flesh, and my mother was screaming 'How dare you! How DARE you!!'

Had Mr Hyde actually raised his hand and struck his wife? No – the opposite had happened, as became clear from his now audible querulous rambling.

'That's all right, then, that's all right. You know you can hit me in the face and get away with it. You know that any other man whose wife hit him in the face would strike her hard on the chest. That's what he'd do – he'd strike her hard ON THE CHEST! But you, you know that you can...'

'Ah, shut up! SHUT UP!!'

'That's right – hit me again – you know you can get away with it, although any other man...'

My mother returned to the dining room, breathing heavily and muttering 'the cheek of him, the cheek of him!' Then we heard our father emerge into the hall, heard the front door open and close, and knew that he had departed into the night.

Sometimes he telephoned on the first or second night of his binge to inform us that he was OK, that we should not worry about him, and that he would be in touch before long. On these occasions, I believe, he would book himself into Moran's Hotel in Talbot Street (not far from his workplace, the Department of Social Welfare in the Central Bus Station) or the Central Hotel in Exchequer Street.

The final incident that I wish to recall occurred after he had been absent for most of a week. On this occasion, there was no violence and no recrimination. He sat down heavily at the supper table and silently ate a few morsels that my mother, just as wordlessly, set before him. Then he lumbered upstairs to the toilet. Another of those long weighty silences followed.

'Run up and see if he's all right,' my mother told me.

Reluctantly, I obeyed. The door of the toilet was ajar. My father, who read Russian magazines, could recite Goethe in the original and argue passionately about Voltaire, sat slumped on the lavatory bowl, his trousers around his ankles, snoring loudly amidst the stench of his own excrement.

No child should have to see such a thing.

Despite these shadows, my life now settled into an almost contented regime of peaceful regularity. Once a week the Correspondence College would send me lessons involving grammar and prescribed texts (and their musical equivalents), as well as sets of questions that I would dutifully answer and return. The lessons done, I would take Rebel for a modest walk in the direction of Drumcondra or Marino. This unwelcome duty fulfilled, I could devote the rest of my time to playing the piano, composing, listening, reading and writing. I had read Kafka's *Journals* and, fired by the spirit of emulation, bought a succession of large hardbound notebooks that I filled over the next couple of years with diary entries, the beginnings of short stories, novels, poems (rarely) and 'philosophical' ruminations of an undoubtedly puerile and embarrassing nature.

Already my sister had caused upheaval in the household by blurting out that she was an atheist and would no longer be attending Mass. Our parents were unanimous: 'We would rather you were dead than that you'd tell us something like that!' Although I had no burning sense of religious conviction, I was still wary of cutting links with The Faith. Our parents' severe reaction, although primarily rhetorical in nature, further deterred me from contemplating such a step. Patsy, however, expected unconditional fraternal support and was disgusted that I took refuge in cowardly silence.

ڪ   ڪ   ڪ

In the summer of 1968 I travelled to Italy. Mario B., a Jesuit friend of my brother Declan's, had been asked by a Milanese family if he could recommend an Anglophone boy to assist their ten-year-old son with his English for a month. I am surprised that I agreed to take on this task, given that it entailed *responsibility*, but my parents agreed that it would be good for me, and Mario (who was, after all, a priest) had reassured them that that the Bavas were a pious Catholic family.

The Bavas' apartment in Via Giulianova was luminous and luxurious in a minimalist, modernist style that was quite unfamiliar to me. Signora Bava, who was alone when I arrived, was a bony woman in her forties. She taught French, in which language we communicated with some difficulty occasioned by my lack of spoken fluency (although by now I could read the language tolerably well) and her entirely Italianate pronunciation, which she presumably passed on to generations of pupils.

My charge, Gianluigi, known as GeGe, already looked like a miniature version of the film star Marcello Mastroianni. He was evidently the sun around which the household orbited. Although spoilt to an almost comical degree, it was to his credit that he proved thoroughly good-natured and more solicitous than either of his parents to make me feel welcome and at ease.

Signor Bava, a portly man some years older than his wife, arrived home from work eager to impress his shy and gauche guest. Comfortably sipping a cognac, he pointed out his most treasured cultural trophy: a portrait by an artist 'from the school of Guido Reni' (a seventeenth century Bolognese master) hanging over the purely ornamental fireplace. '*Gli occhi!*' ('the eyes!'), he exclaimed ecstatically, brandishing his cigar in the direction of the orbs in question. Given that they were the only features discernible amid the unrestored painting's oily murk, I could indeed admire them with complete sincerity.

My teaching duties were light, mostly entailing chatting with GeGe about his greatest interest in life: airplanes, and everything connected with them. Much time was spent teaching him to say 'parachute' and, worse still, 'parachutist'. If I succeeded, I hope the lesson was of some use to him in later life.

A month later it was with some relief that I boarded a train from Milan to Parma, where I was met by Mario B. and conducted to the local headquarters of the Jesuits.

Mario, it turned out, was a socialist whose views on the Bavas were so jaundiced that I silently wondered why he had introduced them to me in the first place. I had no real idea what a socialist was, although I knew that to my parents' nostrils the very word gave off a whiff of sulphur. Eager to introduce me to 'the *real* people', Mario took me to dine with some friends of his, a working-class family. While a meal of many courses was consumed, and a vociferous and presumably political discussion raged between Mario and our hosts, I was plied with homemade red wine, my first taste of alcohol. A few sips alleviated my shyness, and soon my incomprehension of the surrounding clamour seemed a minor irrelevancy. Half way through the first glass, I became convinced that my hosts were the most delightful and humorous people I had encountered in Italy (which may well have been the case) or anywhere else. Once my second glass had been poured, with jovial expressions of encouragement from all corners of the large table, I decided that Mario was right: socialism really was the answer.

By the time we took our leave I had drunk three brimming glasses of the powerful stuff. I was not drunk, but felt at one with the universe and even with myself. I regaled Mario, who hitherto had apparently regarded me as a rather colourless specimen, with a mimicry of one of the more pompous priests to whom he had introduced me in the Jesuit HQ. This reduced him to laughter and evoked the double-edged compliment that I was 'livelier than he had thought'.

The raging and irremediable thirst that affected me next morning did nothing to neutralise the glow in which the previous evening was bathed, or to suggest that this was the first station on a lengthy Calvary along which I would struggle for another twenty years.

ﺱ ﺱ ﺱ

Later that year a call went out for submissions from young composers for inclusion in the first Dublin Festival of Twentieth Century Music. I was composing a new piano work at the time, influenced by Pierre Boulez's *Third Sonata*, a work that allows the pianist some freedom in determining its overall form. Glorying in the then fashionably abstract title *Format I*, the piece was chillingly austere. In the best Boulezian tradition it was unfinished, and in my own tradition I lost the manuscript at some point over the next few years.

The audition took place in the music department of Trinity College, known affectionately as No. 5. Given what struck me – not always justly – as the conservative nature of the other entrants' submissions, I was pleasantly surprised to be successful. On the one hand, I was convinced that this proved my natural superiority; on the other, I believed that my status as the token *avant-garde* composer would continue to work to my advantage.

One Ita Mallon wrote in the *Irish Independent* on 3 January 1969 that 'the youngest of the five composers, Raymond Deane, a native of County Mayo, has composed a wind quartet, a string quartet, songs and a number of piano pieces. His age is a ripe fifteen.'

The article is illustrated with a number of photographs, including one captioned *Rehearsal in the TCD Music Dept* featuring four of the young composers (Derek Ball is missing) and three instrumentalists. I look particularly gormless with my shapeless shock of brown hair, my prim scowl, and my skimpy tie tucked under a schoolboyish pullover. It is hard to imagine untruths escaping the tightly pursed lips of such a nerd, but then how did Ms Mallon come up with my apocryphal songs and quartets? Maybe I imparted intentions as realities, or maybe she engaged in a little creative elaboration of her own.

The day of the concert was unseasonably bright and warm, and the great bay window behind the performers in Trinity's ancient Exam Hall was slightly open. With the most perfunctory of bows, I seated myself at the grand piano and embarked on *Format I*. All went well until a gentle zephyr wafted through the window and brushed the large loose pages of manuscript on to the floor. I heaved myself off the piano stool and, without casting an eye in the direction of the sizeable audience, gathered up the scattered leaves, replaced them on the music stand and continued playing. The warm round of applause I received at the end was as much a vote of sympathy as of appreciation, but no matter! – I was launched, and nothing could stop me now.

Chapter 13

My solitary studies continued apace. I was soundly be-
rated by one of my remote tutors for having dared to
write an essay condemning Edward Burke's view of the French
Revolution. On the basis of the celebrated passage beginning,
'It is now sixteen or seventeen years since I saw the Queen of
France,' I expressed strong disapproval of Burke's distaste for
the common people and his willingness to ignore their sufferings at the hands of pampered royalty. My tutor thought this a
perfectly acceptable opinion for a mature political commenta-
tor to express, but a crass impertinence coming from a green
teenager. I was to confine myself to summarising Burke's point
of view and explaining why his lofty style was so admirable.

As I read this critique of my critique I literally blushed. I
felt both demoralised and indignant, but bit back my pride and
followed the tutor's wise if cynical advice both then and in the
Matriculation examination. I sat this in the Examination Hall
of University College Dublin, located at that time in Earlsfort
Terrace. I passed without difficulty, but was fifteen days too
young to be admitted to University and thus was condemned
to another year of morose dog-walking, and ever more total
immersion in my music, my reading and writing, and myself.

That August I attended the legendary 'vacation courses for
new music' in the small German city of Darmstadt which, in

the 1950s and early 1960s, had become the improbable power-house of the international *avant-garde*. I did not care that by 1969 Darmstadt was already in decline: I was in the presence of such heroes as Ligeti, Maderna and Karlheinz Stockhausen who had so strongly influenced my two lost piano pieces.

Twice daily Stockhausen and his ensemble performed pieces from his new work *From the Seven Days*, a score of which I had purchased on the day of my arrival.

But what was this? The 'score' was a small booklet in land-scape format containing no musical symbols of any sort but consisting of short texts exhorting the reader/performer to play 'a sound with the certainty that you have an infinite amount of time and space', or 'all the rhythms that you can distinguish today between the rhythm of your smallest particles and the rhythm of the universe'. Furthermore, the curiously punctu-ated text *Arrival* exhorted us to 'give everything up, we were on the false path, begin with yourself, you are a musician, you can transform all of the vibrations of the world into sounds.'

I chose to interpret all this rather simplistically: conven-tionally notated music was a thing of the past, 'intuitive mu-sic' – not to be confused with mere 'improvisation' – was the path of and to the future. This was a distressing conclusion that reduced to irrelevance both my own music and the rest of the works being performed in Darmstadt that summer, most of which were more or less traditionally notated.

I arrived early for each day's sessions so that I could seat myself as near to the magnetic Stockhausen as possible. I re-solved to grow my hair long like his, and transferred my part-ing from the left side, where it felt natural, to the right, where it did not, but where Stockhausen had his. I already wore white trousers and shirts, although, unlike my hero, I changed them as rarely as possible and hence their whiteness was severely compromised. I cursed the fact that my eyes were blue rather than brown, and that my voice lacked his reedy baritone resonance. This attitude bordered on the kind of worship that I had never bestowed on any pop stars, not even the yodelling Frank Ifield.

I had signed up for the piano master classes given by one Alfons Kontarsky. I was shocked to find that several of the other young pianists had clearly already mastered the set pieces by Günther Becker, at that time Professor of Composition in Düsseldorf; I had assumed that they would be starting from scratch. I would willingly have stayed in the shadows, but, as ill luck would have it, I was the only person to have secured a copy of Charles Ives's monumental *Concorde Sonata,* another set piece. I was therefore obliged to expose myself to these frighteningly accomplished young specialists and the gimlet-eyed Kontarsky.

'Had I learned the entire Sonata?' asked the latter incredulously.

'No, just the opening pages and the third movement.'

The reality was that I had learned *none* of the piece in the rigorous sense intended by Kontarsky. This rapidly became evident as I launched into *Emerson*, the first movement, only to be stopped after a few bars by a chuckling Kontarsky, amid general sympathetic amusement.

'Oh, I think that is a little too difficult, and needs too much work. Let us hear *Ze Alcotts...*'

The third movement is indeed a much simpler and plainer piece, and I was allowed to play almost half of the first page before Kontarsky stopped me.

'Thank you, thank you, but there are some problems. Those repeated eight-notes at the beginning are not staccato – there is a slur – like so many passages in Schubert's *Sonatas*, you know?'

I did not know, but nodded wisely.

'Please continue...'

I continued, but after a few bars he stopped me again.

'No, no, those chords in the left hand must not be broken...'

'I have to break them – my hand is too small.'

'Then you must not attempt to play this piece.'

He then sat down and played *The Alcotts* from start to finish, note-perfect, rhythm-perfect, to great acclaim. However, a Canadian composer, who happened to be sharing my hotel room, intervened in the ensuing discussion in a manner that went some way towards saving my blushing face.

'Ives wasn't a German composer – he was evoking amateur music-making in a New England drawing room in the mid-nineteenth century. He'd probably have been content to have those chords broken...'

Kontarsky was displeased with this contribution, and peremptorily brought the session to a close.

Subsequently I decided that the failure of the German piano students even to purchase Ives's revolutionary but very American masterpiece proved that they saw it as quaint and irrelevant, compared to Becker's *avant-garde* clichés. Although I felt embarrassed by my misunderstanding of what a 'master class' entailed, and humiliated by the public exposure of my amateurism, I felt vindicated by these reflections on the Germans' narrow-minded and parochial dogmatism. This comforting alibi took the place of engagement with a critique that I chose to take personally: an unfair assault on my vulnerable and fragile self-esteem.

On a social level Darmstadt proved a difficult experience, although it had its bright moments.

My Canadian roommate introduced me to a small, wiry man called Clarence Barlow.

Canadian composer (respectfully): 'Clarence is from India.'

Myself (enthusiastically): 'Oh, really?'

Clarence (sharply): 'It's in the same world, isn't it?'

After this inauspicious beginning, things improved when Clarence learned that I was Irish. It turned out that he had been taught by the Irish Christian Brothers in Calcutta, and could quote sizeable gobbets of the same green-covered Catechism from which I had learned the dogmas of the One True Church. He could also quote reams from Joyce's *Finnegans Wake* and *Ulysses*, so our conversation rapidly took a congenial turn. In the days and evenings that followed, surrounded as we were by monomaniacs of *Neue Musik* (a phrase that means both more and less than 'new music'), this turn became even more congenial and has remained so for more than forty years.

One of these conversations took place in the Schlosskeller, a focal point of nightlife for participants in the Holiday Courses. I had been in the habit of drinking a bottle of beer with my solitary lunches in the canteen, and as yet felt no urge to keep swilling the stuff all day. Now, for the first time, I allowed myself to be bought a couple of vodkas in the course of a stimulating evening in a dimly lit space where my persistent acne was all but invisible. A good night's sleep and a morning without negative consequences completed the illusion that I could be a 'normal' drinker. I made a mental note of the potentially treacherous link between sociability, disinhibition and good cheer. Surely there could be no connection between such conviviality and the memory of my defeated father snoring astride the toilet bowl?

Back in Ireland, I pursued the consequences of my new conviction that 'we were on the false path': no more written composition. I removed the front of the piano, thus gaining direct access to the strings, and spent hours each day attempting to recreate on this humble instrument the sounds I had heard emanating from Stockhausen's high-tech ensemble. Sometimes I meditated on the texts from *From the Seven Days*, seeking vainly to transform the rhythms of my smallest particles into those of the universe, while my family gritted their teeth in the neighbouring room.

A telephone call from Telefís Éireann, Ireland's national broadcaster, conveyed the request that I should play my *Format I* on a children's TV programme called *Motley*. I rather haughtily replied that I had discarded the piece. I was asked if I had anything else to submit for consideration? Fortunately, my iron principles did not push me to insist that 'we were on the wrong path', and a sudden intuition led me to offer them a non-existent new piece that would receive its world premiere on the show.

Instead of jumping at this privilege, my interlocutor told me to show up for audition the following week at the broadcaster's headquarters above the General Post Office in O'Connell Street. Here I met Colm O Briain, *Motley*'s producer, and co-founder (in 1966) of the Project Arts Centre. I played a short piece that I had rustled up for the occasion, and it was duly accepted. Next day I went to the TV studios in Montrose, recorded the as yet untitled piece, and was interviewed by *Motley*'s presenter Jim Sheridan, subsequently a celebrated Hollywood film director.

The new piece set out as an essay in uncompromising dissonance, but for the hell of it I dropped a chord of C major into the mix towards the end, followed by a descending succession of reasonably euphonious chords. The piece ended with a sly harmonic gesture that both negated what went before while producing an ambiguous sense of closure. I did not realise it, but the template for everything I would subsequently compose was in place, if a little awkwardly.

Although I reverted for a time to improvisation, the call for submissions to the second Dublin Festival led me to abandon my wilting principles definitively and write a companion to the *Motley* composition, now officially entitled *Orphic Piece I*. I had been reading about the pagan rituals of Orphism, featuring the dismemberment of Dionysus/Zagreus and his rebirth after Zeus ingests his heart. I thought of myself, a little pompously, as 'dismembering' musical language and 'regenerating' it by recycling the familiar among the unfamiliar. I borrowed an image from Stockhausen, who had compared the presence of a boy's voice within the electronic universe of his *Song of the Youths* to 'finding an apple or an ashtray on a distant star'. In due course this schematic opposition begged a lot of questions (what happens when the distant star becomes familiar?), but for the moment it helped clarify myself to myself.

In the Young Composers' Concert of the 1970 Festival, my *Orphic Piece II* was warmly applauded despite the absence of any wind-induced disasters. My father, to preempt such an accident, had glued each page of manuscript to a piece of cardboard; I had still not discovered the virtues of photocopying.

In the *Irish Independent* Mary McGoris wrote that my piece 'was so much on one note that it sounded like a transcription of a piece for timpani'. This, my first negative review, was in itself a kind of milestone.

ॐ   ॐ   ॐ

That summer I went to London, staying in Cousin Jerry's tiny North London bedsit while he sought new employment in Dublin.

I eventually found work as hall porter in the Whitehall Hotel, Bloomsbury Square, on a weekly salary of £11.00 net. I was provided with an ill-fitting and ill-smelling navy blue jacket that had apparently not been cleaned since worn by my predecessor.

My duties entailed bringing the hefty luggage of departing guests from their rooms, finding taxis for them, helping incoming guests to their rooms in the antiquated lift, bringing them afternoon tea or coffee and biscuits, toting their clothes to and from the cleaners, explaining the new decimal currency to them (while keeping silent when they mistook fifty pence for ten pence coins when tipping me), giving them directions despite knowing almost as little about the gigantic city as themselves, dusting the furniture in the lobby and polishing the banisters, table tops and any other amenable surfaces.

In my spare hours, I soaked up London's cultural life. I went to films, concerts, operas and one ballet (consisting of two dance pieces by Peter Maxwell Davies, a recent hero of mine), and despaired of the contrast between these riches and the poverty of the Dublin scene.

Most memorable was a day of poetry readings in the Queen Elizabeth Hall. This featured a remarkable galaxy of celebrated figures including Allen Tate, Tennessee Williams and Pier Paolo Pasolini. The presenter Patrick Garland read some poems by Paul Celan, who had committed suicide a few months previously; I was stunned, and captured for life. Pasolini, excruciatingly shy, had to be coaxed onstage by the ultra suave Garland, only to flee into the wings at the sight of the capacity audience. Having been retrieved almost forcibly, he mumbled a very lengthy poem in Italian of which the only word I could recognise was, repeatedly, *fascismo*. A very shaky Williams embarrassed the audience by claiming he had just been released from a mental hospital, and complained about having been provided with insufficiently strong tranquillisers. Those, indeed, were the days.

ڪ   ڪ   ڪ

Returning to the bedsit on my penultimate night in London, I was accosted on my way up the stairs by a middle-aged Irishman.

'Are you the lad staying in Jerry Cassidy's flat?'

'I am indeed, but I'm leaving tomorrow.'

'Oh are you now? Then you'll join us for a farewell drink!'

I was ushered into a smoky living room where a bleary-eyed woman of a certain age nodded her head in time to some sentimental Irish ballad wheezing from a tape recorder. Introductions completed, I was handed a pint bottle of Guinness and subjected to a friendly interrogation.

My hosts had spent many years in London without spreading their wings outside the Irish ghetto of Archway. They did not hate the English, but had as little as possible to do with them. London-based Irish newspapers, sentimental and patriotic Irish ballads and Céilí dance music, Guinness stout and Paddy whiskey constituted the backbone of their existences in this alien country that could no longer be entirely blamed for the depressed conditions back home that had forced them to emigrate. The generalised resentment that racked them was all the more bitter for lacking a clear focus.

Why did I not politely bid my two compatriots goodnight after the first bottle of stout? Because, halfway through it, I realised that I would be wanting another one, which was duly forthcoming. Once I had consumed a third one, I was delighted to accept my first ever glass of whiskey. The first few mouthfuls were torture, but before long the taste had mellowed, just as I had mellowed to the point where I was singing along with my host's rendition of *A Nation Once Again* and *The Old Bog Road*.

But why wasn't 'herself' joining in? Was she asleep? Indeed she was, curled up in her armchair, her mouth gaping open, through which the occasional snore or moan escaped into the smoky air...

I was on my feet, not quite sure where the door was, not quite sure where I was, and what was my host pressing into my hand? An orange? It'll do you good!

I was staggering up the stairs, stumbling into the lavatory, vomiting Guinness and Paddy and passively inhaled cigarette smoke and sentimental ballads and London Irishry, and panting, and sweating and vomiting some more.

And now I was lying fully clothed on my bed, seeking to bite off the top of the orange that would do me good, bringing the fruit towards my mouth, miscalculating the distance and the speed and the air, dealing myself a hard blow on the nose with the orange that would do me good...

I awoke next morning with my first real hangover, my first real sensation of post-alcoholic embarrassment and anxiety. As I struggled through the grey day, my last day in London, I was certain of one thing: I had learned my lesson. I would not turn out like my father. I would never drink again.

Chapter 14

I started university in the autumn of 1969. At first I planned to take a Bachelor of Arts degree in music, English and philosophy. Three years' absence from school, however, had not prepared me for the shock of lecture halls filled with as many as 500 students of my own age. I had dandruff and acne, and sought to counteract the latter by rubbing talcum powder on my face, which must have given me a most peculiar look. I sweated a lot and was afraid to look my peers, particularly the female ones, in the eye. Slowly but surely I would learn to deal with these discomforts, but for the time being I was a mess.

Philosophy entailed wading through Plato's *Theaetaetus* with a view to arriving ultimately at Thomas Aquinas.

English involved reading a number of novels that were of no interest to me whatever, including Saul Bellow's *Herzog* and Conrad's notoriously uninvolving *Nostromo*. Reputedly Nabokov's precious *Lolita* had been removed from the syllabus after an organised campaign by parents anxious to preserve the innocence of their offspring. Another version had it that a delegation of first year students – from 'down the country', of course – had themselves requested its withdrawal.

Music lectures were held in a distant corner of the Arts complex. My year boasted only a couple of dozen students of whom it was assumed, correctly, that many would fall by the wayside. The campus was no longer located in Earlsfort Terrace, but in Belfield, several miles south of the city centre. Living as I did on the Northside, and with many music lectures starting at 9.00 a.m. that first year, I had no choice but to rise at 7.00, something of a shock to my rather cosseted system.

The Professor, Anthony Hughes, lectured on the set works, including Schubert's song cycle *Die schöne Müllerin* and works by Mozart and Tchaikovsky. A slightly tense relationship was established between us from the start, not enhanced (as he confided to a friend of mine some years later) by my habit of keeping a solitary sheet of paper in front of me on which I rarely wrote any notes, and sometimes folded and replaced in my pocket well before the lecture had ended. While other students rose to first name terms in his dry affections, I would remain 'Mr Deane' throughout my university apprenticeship.

I began to attend choir practice in Newman House on St. Stephen's Green, a lovely old building that was still used by the University. I had no interest in choral singing, but thought that this might be an opportunity to meet girls. In this I was disappointed, but I met a number of boys who were interested in discussing girls over a few pints in Hartigans of Leeson Street afterwards. Among these were Paul, a prospective composer, and Conall who, seven years older than myself, was the daddy of us all and a man-about-town in the best possible sense.

My most diligent classmate was Patrick (Paddy) Devine, whom I forgave his attachment to the music of Shostakovich because he was willing to listen patiently to my enthusiastic harangues about the superior merits of Stockhausen. One evening he invited me to a lecture on modern music, to be given by the composer and broadcaster Brian Boydell. This took place under the auspices of the Austrian Society in the Shelbourne Hotel on St. Stephen's Green. The audience consisted mainly of demure fur-clad women and their dapper consorts, most of them Austrian; I no longer recall how Paddy came to have invitations.

I listened with growing outrage as the genial and eloquent Professor posited Sibelius and Bartok as the greatest modern composers, before pooh-poohing the 'artificiality' of Schoenberg's techniques and playing an extract from Stockhausen's *Song of the Youths* which, he declared derisively, was invalidated by the fact that it reminded 'one' of digestive noises.

I was nervously determined to make a derogatory comment, but inhibited from so doing until Paddy broke the ice by asking the speaker's opinion of Shostakovich.

'He's written some very fine things, I'll admit, but much of his music reminds me of those grandiose monuments to Lenin and Stalin one sees everywhere behind the Iron Curtain...'

Tentatively I put my hand up. My voice trembling, I expressed my conviction that the learned Professor knew nothing about contemporary music, and that his remarks about Stockhausen were both an insult to that most significant of living composers and to the audience. After the inevitable sharp intakes of breath there ensued an uneasy silence, before the discussion was rapidly terminated. I made good my escape into the winter night, my cheeks aflame.

It was impossible to feel proud of what had just occurred, much though I might have wished to. True, I had 'unmasked' a kind of imposture, as I saw it, yet what had this achieved? Were any of these people likely to take my intervention seriously? Was the Professor likely to reform his views of contemporary music, to which he was fully entitled? Had I not merely been priggish and ungracious, and in the process done more harm than good?

I recalled that Conall, who lived near Belfield, had said he came into town for a few drinks in the Grafton Mooney every Thursday. Today was Thursday, and Grafton Street was just around the corner. Fearing that I might have fled the frying-pan to take refuge in the fire, yet too agitated to contemplate the next bus home, I entered the pub, the first time in my life I had done such a thing on my own.

I immediately spotted Conall's blond mop amidst a group of drinkers at the end of the bar. Rather than impose myself on these people without warning, I bought a bottle of ale – my London experience had frightened me off Guinness for the time being – and hovered around 'nonchalantly' until Conall noticed me and invited me to join the company.

These people were all of Conall's age, hence seemed to belong to a different generation. The men all had those rather bouffant 1970s hairstyles that were beyond my power to imitate, and wore luxuriant moustaches (my own was but a wisp). They sported colourful pullovers, from the necks of which sprang the wing-like collars of their immaculate shirts. They wore bell-bottom jeans over buckled shoes or high-heeled boots. They brandished their pints with well-practised ease. They chain-smoked, and smelled of aftershave and body spray.

The women, fewer in number, ignored me so comprehensively that I could save face only by ignoring them, a stance made easier by their advanced age.

Conall was genial and, although surprised to see me, solicitous to make me feel at ease and amused by my graphic account of the Shelbourne debacle. He bought me a pint – bottles were strictly for the birds, he said – and someone else bought me another one. I drank, chatted and did not outstay my welcome.

I had survived this difficult social encounter without disaster, thus setting a further ominous precedent: drink was an entrance ticket to sociability; it relaxed inhibitions; it calmed the nerves after (and, as I would discover, before) tense situations. The ice had been broken, and would be broken repeatedly until I began to sink beneath it.

ৎ   ৎ   ৎ

The central bus station, on the top floor of which my father's branch of the Department of Social Welfare was located, was built in the year of my birth in the 'International Modern' style. It was a glass building, but the windows could not be opened and there was no functioning air conditioning. One after the other, my father saw his workmates succumb to respiratory ailments and heart disease. He may have felt that this insalubrious work environment was 'driving him to drink'; he never acknowledged that drink was doing the driving.

Alarmed at his increasing depression, my mother had written to his superior protesting at the lack of recognition for his years of loyal and scrupulous service. Although this scrupulosity was itself one of the obstacles to his advancement, the boss felt impelled to make a gesture and moved him up a notch. But he had been Manager in Achill Sound, and remained at a lower grade even after this promotion. Realising that no further concessions would be forthcoming, he took early retirement in 1970, aged 62.

While the decision had financial consequences for the family – which, for a time, he and Jackie (or John, as I must now call him) sought to alleviate by giving language lessons and calling themselves the North City Language Centre – it was undoubtedly the right one, as his dipsomaniac absences became less and less frequent.

By Christmas I decided to discard English and philosophy, and henceforth concentrate on music. Once again I had taken an escape route, reducing both my social and academic options while convincing myself that I was merely setting aside more time for composition.

In the *Feis Ceoil* the following spring, I competed in the Nordell Cup, playing Alban Berg's *Piano Sonata*. The adjudicator was Ronald Smith, an English concert pianist I greatly admired. Smith gave me a 'highly commended' mention which, while disappointing, was not entirely discouraging. Furthermore, a photograph of me appeared in the *Evening Press* newspaper (now defunct), the caption of which flatteringly described me as a 'lean Mayo man'. I was happy.

Entering a new academic year, I was no longer the same shy, acne-ridden, talcum-powdered freak as before. However, my shyness and freakishness had merely been pushed under the surface, which had begun to acquire a sophisticated veneer that would all too often function as a kind of armour.

My drinking seemed under control, and had certainly played a role in enhancing my sociability. Not long after term began, however, its ominous side materialised. The music department held a wine and cheese party in Newman House, at which I hoped to impress eligible female students with my new trendy tinted glasses and my hard-learned debonair ways.

Concluding that none of the women were worth pursuing, and having no great taste for cheese, I soon concentrated my attention on the wine.

The party over, I repaired with the usual suspects – and a few hangers-on, as I thought of them – to the upstairs lounge of O'Dwyer's pub in Leeson Street. Here I unwisely graduated to beer. By the time we moved across the road to Hourican's I was fast losing my grip. Later in the evening, realising that all was not well with my innards, I staggered down the stairs to the men's toilet just in time to fall on my knees and disgorge the contents of my stomach into the WC.

This was the good news. The bad news was that my new tinted glasses flew off my nose into the same receptacle. My head having cleared somewhat, there was nothing for it but to fish them out and wash off the foul matter. When I replaced them on my nose, I realised that the right lens had acquired a jagged crack.

Until closing time I huddled quietly in a corner of the pub while my friends chatted and caroused. When the session moved to a flat in Rathgar or Rathmines I allowed myself to be put to bed, having begun to shudder uncontrollably. At three in the morning my hostess woke me and, after cleaning myself up, I took a taxi home.

This incident was like a more horrible sequel to the dreary disaster in London, with added public exposure and consequently a deeper sense of shame. Nonetheless, my parents seemingly turned a blind eye to this plain evidence of advancing depravity, perhaps lulled into tolerance by the fact that the previous evening's debauch had been an official university social event. Even the replacement of my expensive tinted glasses with their untinted predecessors, which I had fortunately retained, provoked no awkward questions. For some time my parents would obstinately keep their heads in the sand, but I am sure that deep down they suffered much anxiety.

Back in college, I was teased about my collapse, but in a manner that implied it had been something wild and bohemian rather than sordid and pathetic. I should have eaten more cheese; I shouldn't have mixed red and white wine; I shouldn't have mixed grape and grain. I would, of course, know better in future! It was also clear that certain predictable assumptions had been made about my having lingered in our hostess's flat after everyone else had left. I did not contradict these myths but smiled knowingly.

When *Feis Ceoil* time came around again in the spring of 1972, I worked hard to prepare the fiendishly difficult *Piano Sonata No.10* by Alexander Scriabin for the Nordell Cup, even memorising it thoroughly, as I thought.

Disaster struck early. In the slow introduction I experienced a memory blackout, requiring a few seconds' frantic improvisation before I got back on track. Convinced that I had already excluded myself from consideration, I relaxed and resolved to play only for myself. When the sonata's astonishing climax arrived I experienced – for the first and only time during a public performance – that 'state of fugue' so familiar to real pianists. When I emerged from it, the climax behind me, I sensed a rapt quality in the audience's attention, a feeling that was confirmed by the warmth of the lengthy round of applause when I had finished.

Ah yes, but surely this was just a vote of sympathy for the calamitous memory lapse! When the adjudicator Harry Isaacs, a professor at London's Royal Academy, announced that I had won, I gazed about me in an uncomprehending daze and had to be pushed by my brother John to step forward and accept the cup.

A few evenings later I played the sonata again in the Prize-winners' Concert. I played it well, entirely without memory lapses, but the earth never moved. The high point of my pianistic career was behind me.

Emboldened by the warm public reaction to the Young Composers' Concerts, a group of us decided to duplicate the experiment outside of the Festival context. Instigated by Brian Beckett, a piano teacher in the Royal Irish Academy of Music and a composer of – he would be the first to admit – highly conservative leanings, the trial run was a Saturday afternoon concert in the Trinity College Exam Hall. We decided optimistically that the profits would take half a dozen of us to Bayreuth to see and hear Wagner's *Ring des Nibelungen.*

The concert was reasonably well attended – by today's standards, one would describe the attendance as large – but the profits, once the hall, the piano and various fees were deducted, barely sufficed to buy us all a few drinks in Kennedy's Pub in Westland Row. Evidently a certain dislocation from reality was not unique to myself.

Nothing daunted, our hard core (Beckett, Derek Ball, Gerald Barry, John Gibson, Jerome de Bromhead, Niamh O'Kelly and myself – a predominantly masculine clique, I fear) set up the Association of Young Irish Composers (AYIC), for which the same pub served as an office, with Saturday evenings earmarked as the best time for meetings.

These were, naturally, bibulous and sometimes fractious affairs. On one occasion, harassed beyond measure by my persistent singing of a theme from his *Piano Sonata* to the words 'Chim-chiminey, Chim-chiminey, Chim-chim cheroo' from the musical *Mary Poppins,* Beckett extinguished his cigarette on the back of my right hand. There was a ruthless quality to the derision I heaped upon anything that fell short of my modernist precepts; clearly, conservatism could retaliate with equal ruthlessness.

After the meetings Gerald Barry, who lived in Phibsboro, on the Northside, would give me a lift home on the pillion of his primitive motorbike. This I found terrifying, less because Gerald was rarely quite sober on these occasions than because of my own tendency to lean in the opposite direction to whichever turn we were taking, thus threatening to upend us both. On our first trip I rested my left foot on the exhaust pipe, until a pungent smell alerted me to the fact that it was burning through the sole of my shoe.

For all its bohemianism, the AYIC rapidly carved out a niche for itself, particularly with 'portrait' concerts featuring the works of one or two composers at a time. At first these concerts were held in the Exam Hall, but later branched out to St Catherine's Church in Thomas Street, not far from Guinness's Brewery and Jonathan Swift's 'House for Fools and Mad', St Patrick's Hospital. Charles Acton, the music critic of the *Irish Times,* strongly disapproved of the whole venture, considering that we were implicitly cold shouldering our elder and better composer colleagues. If anything, his disapproval was viewed as an accolade.

ڪ   ڪ   ڪ

As I entered the second half of my university career, it seemed as if nothing could stop me. Elected 'auditor' (chairman) of the music society, I was able to programme an enterprising series of lunchtime concerts largely funded by a number of 'popular' evening gigs with groups like Supply, Demand and Curve, featuring long-haired composer Roger Doyle on the drums, and Skid Row, a blues-rock band that had once featured the legendary Phil Lynott on vocals.

The only calamity was a projected concert of recorder music to be played by Michael Dervan, subsequently Charles Acton's successor as music critic of the *Irish Times*, and a mutual acquaintance who shall remain nameless. Given that the programme was to include the world premiere of the latter's *Micturition* (i.e. 'urination') it is possibly just as well that the composer/performer failed to show up. At the last moment Professor Hughes, once a concert pianist of some note, stepped into the breach with two Mozart sonatas for which I dutifully turned the pages. Afterwards, when I publicly thanked him, his nod of acknowledgment with raised eyebrows seemed to say, 'if you *will* insist on inviting your dissolute friends, this kind of thing *will* happen'. Conall and I bought him several pints of lager afterwards in the college bar, but this was not a particularly convivial occasion.

Indeed, I had the impression that he took a generally dim view of myself, my music, my approach to concert programming and just about everything else about me. The lack of harmony between us would come to a head the following year.

If the Professor later commented to a friend of mine that I 'was the first auditor more noted for his drinking than for his musicianship', this may partly have been due to an innovation of which I was particularly proud: the provision of a barrel of beer at the Christmas and Easter parties to supplement the orange squash that had hitherto been the sole liquid staple of those dismal events.

When spring arrived it seemed that my most pressing emotional need was about to be fulfilled: I fell in love! The young woman was blond, as I had always imagined she would be. She was still in secondary school, but mature in manner and apparently so in outlook. She was bright, had a sense of humour, and liked to drink. What's more, she had just split up with a long-time boyfriend, and seemed far from reluctant to fill the vacancy without any delay.

Our entire 'affair' consisted of a few meetings in public houses where we held hands and kissed. On one occasion, to my public mortification but private exultation, we were loudly exhorted by an officious barmaid to 'stop snogging in the corner!'

Within a matter of weeks, this tenuous romance was destroyed before it had a change to get off the ground.

The girl's mother issued an ultimatum: she was sure that I was a person of great talent, but as I already had a reputation as a foul-mouthed drunkard, she felt obliged to forbid her daughter from having anything to do with me. This appeared to have been triggered by a party at which the mother had been present, when I had turned up with a six-pack of beer and had been overheard calling one of my best friends a 'gobshite'.

For a time we defiantly contrived to side-step this prohibition, but when the not-so-long-lost boyfriend reappeared on the scene my wayward beloved decided that he merited a second chance. Suddenly there were no more phone calls from her, and mine went unanswered.

At last a well-meaning mediator arranged a meeting between us in the very bar where our snogging had been discouraged. To my horror, the girl turned up with her best friend who, in fairness to her, seemed unaware that she was to be both chaperone and bodyguard. After some preliminaries, I was told that 'it was not as though there was ever going to be a great idyll between us', that she had realised how committed she was to her former and current boyfriend, and that of course we would always remain the best of friends. Is there a more deadly phrase in existence?

And that was it. From first embrace to final farewell, this interlude had lasted but a single month (the cruellest one: April). Any well-adjusted self-respecting 20-year-old, particularly one with so many positive things happening in his life, would have taken this in his stride. He would, of course, have been downhearted and probably resentful, but he would have picked himself up and moved on.

Not me. It was as if I had encountered an immovable obstacle in my path and quite simply refused to bypass it.

Clearly a great many pent-up impulses, ardent and idealistic as well as sensual, had directed themselves towards this unsuspecting young woman. Her behaviour was less than perfect, perhaps, but she was only seventeen and could hardly be expected to realise just what weighty aspirations had been invested in her. Anyway, my shyness and inexperience had prevented me from expressing my feelings openly, and from behaving at any point in a decisive rather than a passive, sulky and self-pitying manner.

Perhaps I could nonetheless have weathered this storm had it raged in a teacup rather than a pint glass. Instead, I discovered the fatal joy of drowning my sorrows. In my cups, I would listen to sentimental pop songs until the tears began to flow. I discovered Jacques Brel, and listened over and over to *Ne me quitte pas*, that anthem of abjection that I still cannot hear without distress. I projected myself to my friends as an abandoned lover, eliciting reactions ranging from half-amused sympathy through impatience to ridicule. One friend – the same one I had excoriated as a gobshite – urged me repeatedly to 'stop playing the martyr', a formulation that enraged me but that was surely to the point.

My brother John married Barbara Sheridan in July 1973 and I was best man – but only on paper, because I was clearly not to be trusted with such responsible duties as cutting the cake or making a funny speech. The reception was held in the Royal Marine Hotel, Dún Laoghaire. I drank several pints of Guinness with my brother Declan, who had performed the wedding ceremony and was now displaying considerable dedication to the task of drinking alcohol.

I composed a piece for the piano called *Linos*, 'a lament to the departing summer', although that oppressive season had barely begun. I played it to a couple of indifferent friends at a party that continued into the small hours of the morning. Intercepted by my father as I sneaked home, I lost control of myself completely, accusing him of being the cause of all my woes by handing me down his alcoholic genes. The sight of his distress at this callous shot sobered me very slightly, and I explained my current sorrows to him in some detail. He gently told me that alcohol would do nothing to alleviate my pain and would only make it worse. As he spoke, a moment of rare communication, the dawn chorus made itself heard from Griffith Avenue's plane trees.

'Listen,' said my father, and we stood there in silence for a few moments.

'Life goes on,' he said. 'Now go to bed and sleep it off.'

I started my final year in college, having lost all interest in securing good results. I might have ceased turning up for lectures, were it not for the fact that my heartless beloved had started attending, and I still had some dull hopes that a miracle might occur. As for taking action to bring about such a miracle, as the gobshite persistently advised, nothing was further from my mind. Indeed, my behaviour was hardly calculated to bring about a reconciliation: whenever I encountered her I scowled and turned away, responding to her salutations with a silent sneer.

At last Professor Hughes summoned me to his office and told me that, as I had not attended the quota of lectures, he would not allow me to sit my final exams. I protested that this was unfair, that he should have given me advance warning of my precarious status, and that I was prepared to mend my ways.

Very well, he said. I would have to arrange an interview with the Registrar at which I would explain why I had attended so few lectures, and it would be up to him to decide my fate.

The Registrar was a priest, and a psychologist. He was a pleasant man, whose manner was not authoritarian and whose courtesy was not patronising.

'So why have you not been turning up to lectures, Raymond?'

'For personal reasons, Father.'

'Do these "personal reasons" still pertain?'

'They do, Father.'

'And are you prepared to enlighten me as to their nature?'

'I'm sorry, Father, they're just too personal.'

'And will they continue to affect your attendance?'

'No, Father, I won't let them do that.'

'Are you prepared to write a letter of apology to Professor Hughes, repeating your intention to improve your attendance?'

I was, and I did, and from then on a frosty truce prevailed between myself and the Professor. Another unnecessary crisis had been averted – but only just.

ڪ   ڪ   ڪ

I settled into a regime of sorts. Each day I was in university by 11.00, attended a lecture, and had lunch in the canteen capped by a pint in the bar. After the afternoon lecture I went home, and worked until 6.00. Then I would knock together a snack for myself while my mother prepared dinner, and depart for the pub at around 7.30, leaving my parents to dine without me and, no doubt, wonder where they had gone wrong.

I had ceased to buy gramophone records or books, and had begun selling off those I possessed in order to buy drink. The only books I now read were novels that reflected my tragic experience of unrequited love (from *Mansfield Park* to *Sister Carrie*), or that dealt with alcoholism from within. I read and re-read Malcolm Lowry's *Under the Volcano*, accompanying it with lashings of tequila, a drink I found highly potent and not a little nauseating. F. Scott Fitzgerald's *The Beautiful and Damned* enthralled me, but not as much as *Tender is the Night* which converted me to drinking what I thought of as Manhattans: Scotch and ginger ale.

I became a virtuoso at ferreting out friendly barmen who would let me have an occasional drink on the house, perhaps out of pity.

For the time being I avoided the hair of the dog, the early morning pick-me-up that alleviates a hangover by reviving the previous night's intoxication. Thanks to youth and regular meals, my hangovers were not nearly as intense as they would eventually become.

I had come to loathe Christmas passionately, and that of 1973, coming hot on the heels of my romantic martyrdom, was particularly hard to bear. Unfortunately, Christmas is inevitably followed a week later by the New Year, and in my bleak mood the prospect of 1974 was anything but heartening.

I was going through a phase of dandification at that time, often wearing a grey suit over which I threw a long, elegant beige overcoat donated to me by Declan (I concluded that he had inherited it from a deceased parishioner of means). On New Year's Eve I donned this finery and spent the evening drinking in Conradh na Gaeilge in Harcourt Street, an Irish-speaking club with a particularly boisterous atmosphere. I poured out my sorrows to a sympathetic female friend who poured drink after drink into me.

At midnight I found myself standing on the banks of the River Liffey near the Customs House, tears blurring my vision as I listened to the concert of church bells and ships' sirens ushering out the sad old year. I removed my cherished overcoat and threw it into the murky waters. I removed the almost equally cherished jacket of my suit, containing my wallet, and flung it in the overcoat's wake. I removed the front door key from my pocket and flung it as far as I could into the freezing darkness. Now I had nothing left, no excuse for continuing to live.

I did not jump in, but climbed over the parapet, descended a metal ladder, and pushed myself into the filthy, foul-smelling, freezing water. I was not prepared for the shock of that icy water, and in a trice my head cleared sufficiently for me to recognise that I could not go through with this madness. I swam back to the ladder and hoisted myself to the pavement and the New Year.

Unable to contemplate walking the two or three miles home in my squelching shoes I stood at a taxi rank, dripping and shuddering in my sodden polo-neck and trousers. I was hardly an enticing customer for taxi drivers, and vehicle after vehicle slowed down and sped up again as soon as my condition was noted.

Then a young couple arrived. The man was engrossed in his mate, but she observed my plight and, to his annoyance, asked me what was wrong. When I explained what I had done, the boyfriend snorted and forcefully urged her to leave me to my fate. At that moment a taxi arrived. Ignoring the boyfriend's protests, she marshalled me into the back seat, sat beside me, and put her arm around me to still my trembling. Overcoming an evident desire to storm off, the boyfriend flounced into the passenger seat and maintained a contemptuous silence throughout the journey to Griffith Avenue, where the girl-friend, a Samaritan to the last, saw me to my door and wished me a happy New Year, no irony intended.

I hope this incident did not blight the relationship between these two people. Perhaps one day that compassionate woman will read this narrative and recognise herself, and know that I have never forgotten her kindness, so far beyond what I deserved.

Naturally, my parents were distraught. While my mother exclaimed, over and over, 'What got into you?' my father said nothing but busied himself drawing a hot bath and making a pot of tea. Was he reflecting on those terrible words I had flung at him the previous summer as the songbirds announced dawn, and wondering whether he had indeed played a role – inadvertent, genetic, tragic – in bringing me to such a pass?

Next day I rose in time for lunch, which was eaten in stunned silence. When the telephone rang, it was the female friend with whom I had been drinking the previous evening; she was worried about me, as I had seemed to be in very morbid form. I recounted my subsequent adventures in detail, and not in hushed tones, and we exchanged jokes on the subject. When I returned to the dining table my mother expressed her understandable outrage that I could have spoken so flippantly and even laughed about such an appalling event. As so often, I merely shrugged my shoulders.

Had my parents briefly entertained a glimmer of hope that this experience might somehow bring me to my senses, this shrug must have served as an expressive rebuttal.

Part Three

No more
Like a rat in a corner
No more
Like a bat in a trap
But luminous, humble, triumphant
I accept defeat.

– John Jordan

Chapter 15

Igraduated from UCD with a Bachelor of Music degree (B.Mus) but only succeeded in coming second in my year, behind the diligent Paddy Devine. The next step was to use this qualification as a ticket to make good my escape from Ireland.

My unwary sister Patricia, who had taken up a post as translator for the Bank for International Settlements in Basel, invited me to come and stay with her. I packed my bags, had a series of frenetic farewell drinking sessions, and flew off to Switzerland with an almighty hangover.

Significantly enough, I chose not to 'cure' this condition with a few drinks in Dublin Airport or on the airplane. This expedient had not yet become a habit, but that would change before long.

Patricia's apartment was in the featureless suburb of Allschwil. My bed was the couch in the living room, which also featured a piano, record player and TV. This being Switzerland, I was warned that I was not to touch the piano before 10.00 a.m., between the hours of 12.00 and 2.00 p.m., or after 10.00 p.m. The safest way to listen to records was through headphones, otherwise the volume should be kept acceptably low, a subjective judgment not always shared by our neighbours.

Allschwil was in the canton of Basel-Land and was predominantly Catholic. The Catholic church was nearby; its bells rang out on the hour but also at each quarter. There was also a Lutheran church nearby, with an equally industrious set of bells. However, perhaps subtly nodding to doctrinal differences in an ecumenical age, the two sets of bells were a minute or so out of synch. No sooner would the Papists stop ringing than the Prods would take up the refrain, four times per hour, leaving an insomniac like myself gnashing his teeth and wondering why such a din was considered compatible with stringent anti-noise regulations.

The first weekend in Basel saw my introduction to the Warteck Pub on one of the city's main streets, Steinenvorstadt. This was to become my principal refuge for the next year or so. Part of a chain called 'Pickwick Pubs', it was staffed by Serbs, Englishmen and Scots – not a Swiss to be found. Patricia was well-known to them, and I was welcomed with open arms as her perennially thirsty kid brother.

My composition teacher was the US-born Gerald Bennett. Although only in his early thirties, he had been director of the Conservatoire since 1969. He was a small, balding man with an engaging manner, and we hit it off well. Within a few days he had negotiated a small but (theoretically) adequate scholarship for me from the canton where I lived and, once again, it looked as though nothing could stop me.

Bennett complimented me on the originality of my compositions, but diagnosed an over-reliance on repetition and an absence of complexity, a notion he distinguished from mere complication. He gave me pieces to analyse including an orchestral work by himself, Boulez's first two *Piano Sonatas*, Berio's *Epifanie* for soprano and orchestra, Elliott Carter's *Double Concerto*, and Stockhausen's *Zeitmasse* for woodwind quintet. He was less interested in note-by-note analysis than in the tracing of broader tendencies and transformations.

I threw myself with gusto into this work, and into a number of new, more 'complex' compositions. Simultaneously and unnecessarily, however, I began to lose faith in the works of my first period, dismissing them as mere student works now that, for the first time, I was officially a composition student.

I worked my way through my sister's books including Germaine Greer's *Female Eunuch* and Kate Millett's *Sexual Politics*. I thus convinced myself that I had mastered the theory of feminism, and yearned for the opportunity to put it into practice.

And I drank. I developed the habit of eating a small lunch in the Warteck, usually goulash soup and a roll, followed by a few large beers and a trip to the cinema. If I still had money in my pocket, I would then return to the Warteck and while away the evening discussing films and literature with one or another of the boozy expat would-be intellectuals with whom I rapidly became friendly.

Then came a morning when I fell off my couch in a state that precluded breakfast, work, reading or anything other than dealing with an apocalyptic hangover. I was nauseous, but although I crouched over the toilet bowl and rubbed my stomach hard (I still had not learned the fine art of sticking my fingers down my throat) I could bring up nothing. I was sweating all over, intolerably thirsty with a thirst that water would not slake, my eyes were burning and my hands trembling.

There was beer in the fridge, and I made short work of it. Still feeling shaken, reluctant to face Patricia who was soon due back for lunch, I sprayed deodorant under my armpits and, without showering or shaving, dressed, pocketed a book and left.

I walked unsteadily to the nearest *Gaststätte*, a homely restaurant cum bar just beginning to fill with lunchtime clients.
Seating myself in an inconspicuous corner, I ordered a pint and
took out my book. Three beers later I felt almost human again,
and was able to take a tram into the city and sit through a film.
Later I met Patricia, who as yet seemed unfazed by my behaviour and was willing to join me for dinner and a few drinks.

Days like this were still a rarity, but they would become more
frequent and more incapacitating until there was no other kind
of day and incapacitation was my normal state. Yet when I returned to Dublin that Christmas I felt reasonably pleased with
myself. I had received two months' scholarship at once, so I
was able to swan around town boasting about my glamorous
and sophisticated lifestyle on mainland Europe.

On 14 December the AYIC presented a 'Concert of Works
by Raymond Deane', in which I participated as pianist. This
included *Embers*, a short piece for string quartet that I now
consider to be one of my best works, and *Epilogue* for flute
and piano. Both works had been composed the previous year,
before my graduation from UCD, and I already looked down
my nose at them.

ݺ   ݺ   ݺ

Back in Basel, my lifestyle deteriorated rapidly. I studiously
avoided keeping company with other students from the Conservatoire, who struck me as being too staid and conventional
(although of course I could not know if this was really the case,
since I avoided them). Instead, I hung out with the garrulous
drinkers who socialised in the Warteck, the Atlantis, or *Aux
Balances*. The latter was a particularly louche establishment
characterised by a permanent smell of hashish and by highly

disorientating décor: tables and chairs hung from its ceiling, a mirror image of those on and at which one sat.

The bohemians with whom I kept company all had jobs and hence more money than I did. For the most part they were delighted to buy me drink. The most unhinged of these characters was a sarcastic and argumentative Frenchman called Claude, who worked in the French section of Basel's huge railway station. He was responsible for directing trains on to the right tracks to ensure they didn't collide. Given his habits, that was anything but a comforting thought. Being in possession of a travel pass, after a Friday night's drinking he would, by his own account, simply subside into the nearest train, waking up the next morning in Rome, Paris or Hamburg, where he would continue his binge.

On one occasion, after a lengthy session with Claude, I woke up on my couch fully clothed and with my white jeans covered in bloodstains. After ascertaining that I was uninjured, I showered, changed and, still a little merry, wandered into the city to take up where I had left off, wherever that was.

I strolled into Atlantis where the first person I encountered was Claude, his fine aquiline nose unprepossessingly swathed in a bandage. This, I deduced, was the source of the worrying bloodstains. Apparently he had fallen down the stairs of whatever dive we had ended up in and I had escorted him to hospital. I had no memory of this uncharacteristic piece of Good Samaritanism, but I hope that it really happened and was not yet another of the fabrications in which Claude delighted.

In the early summer of 1975 I completed *Amalgam* for violin and ensemble, much of the final section of which was composed at a table in the Warteck. I attended master classes by the US composer Earle Brown, at the end of which I participated in the student concert that featured the premiere of *Amalgam* as well as works by Brown and other *avant-gardistes.*

In Morton Feldman's very quiet *De Kooning* I played piano and celesta alongside four other musicians, with Brown conducting. I had never touched a celesta before; at one point, when nervously shifting from celesta to piano, I struck a chord rather loudly on the latter. Brown's grimace of disgust has remained with me down the years. I also participated in Lamonte Young's *Poem for Chairs, Tables, Benches etc.* in which Brown and several students imperturbably pushed furniture around the concert hall. This provoked one elderly male audience member to hiss '*prektical chokes!*' and walk out, a reaction that cheered us greatly.

The soloist in *Amalgam* was the brilliant young Canadian violinist Carmen Fournier, who had a distinguished career ahead of her in the world of modern music. The other musicians played with impeccable professionalism. The performance, conducted by Bennett, was well received; afterwards, he and I met in the Warteck and downed so many beers together that my opinion of him soared.

Thus I returned to Ireland that summer in a triumphant mood. My parents had moved to a cottage in Bunclody, County Wexford (actually just over the border in County Carlow), so I stayed mainly with friends in Dartmouth Square, south of the city centre, or with my brother John and his family in Kimmage, still further away from town.

I became besotted with another woman, a very beautiful and rather 'posh' individual who fancied herself as a poet, pianist and singer, but probably had few gifts in any of these domains. She wasn't much of a drinker, and although at first she seems to have found my booziness rather endearing she rapidly came to disapprove of it and me. A tone of mutual recrimination set in early on, so the omens were rather discouraging.

In August I presented a concert of my music at the Project Arts Centre in Dublin's Temple Bar, and repeated it shortly thereafter at the Kilkenny Arts Week, where I was composer of the year. Between these events, I had woken up one morning in the Meath Hospital with several stitches above my right eye. I could not remember what had happened, and a doctor only knew that an ambulance had deposited me there, unconscious, in the small hours of the morning. I had apparently been within a millimetre of losing the eye.

I played the Kilkenny concert wearing an eye-patch, a pinkish, conical affair that gave me neither a rakish nor a piratical air and was highly uncomfortable. By the time I returned to Basel I had shed the patch, but still sported a red cornea that took several weeks to regain its normal colour.

Something had snapped once again, perhaps not unconnected with the fact that my latest paramour had 'betrayed' me with my friend the gobshite, who was doing everything possible to earn his nickname. My relationship with Patricia was growing daily more strained; apart from anything else, she was tiring of the fact that I took up her living room at night and sometimes, at weekends, kept her locked out for much of the day while I sought in vain to sleep off my hangovers.

At last she told me that she could no longer put up with this situation. She found me an attic room in the house of a pleasant family called Meyer, who lived just two tram stops away. She would pay the rent, and I could continue to work in her flat during the day. This rational arrangement did not last very long. During the first week I behaved like a model tenant, but each morning I was awoken at what I thought of as an unearthly hour by the family's two young sons – actually very pleasant lads – getting ready for school.

That weekend I went overboard. Having been drinking steadily in the city, I arrived back at the house at 3.00 or 4.00 a.m., knocked at the parents' bedroom door and abused them loudly in English for allowing their brats to wake me every morning. I staggered to the attic and collapsed fully clothed on the bed.

I was awoken by a small man in a dark suit, flanked by two uniformed giants.

'Have the Nazis invaded?' I fearfully inquired.

I was unceremoniously escorted from the house, while the parents and children looked on anxiously. I was taken to a central police station, kicked around just a little, and locked up for the brief remainder of the night.

Next day, stunned, shaken and anticipating immediate deportation, I was instead given coffee and driven back to the Meyers's house to collect my bags. Good-natured Herr Meyer, instead of heaping well-deserved abuse on my aching head, actually apologised for having called the police. 'But it was for the sake of the children, you understand.' I understood, but I still had the gall to take it amiss, and left with my head in the air. The police, rather considerately under the circumstances, decided not to embarrass me by driving me back to Patricia's. Instead they called a taxi, and the grotesque incident was closed.

My time in Basel dragged on unproductively for a while. At the end of November I flew back to Dublin. I was so overcome with nausea on the early morning flight, despite having breakfasted liberally on brandy, that I was taken off the airplane by an ambulance and delivered to an infirmary in Dublin Airport, where another long-suffering and exasperated sibling collected me and brought me to recuperate in his Kimmage home.

Thus my Swiss interlude, despite the best efforts of so many people to facilitate it, came to a sticky end. Of course I blamed Basel for this. It was inhabited by 'the most boring people in the world', as I wrote in a 1982 article, forgetting that I had made no attempt to acquaint myself with any of its citizens. Indeed, I was barely conscious of the beauties of that ancient city on the Rhine, seeing it merely as a network of bars and nightclubs.

I had obstinately shunned my fellow music students on the grounds that their lives were too narrow and sober, but knew full well that my own way of life was indefensible. Its destructiveness was shown by my decrepit condition at the end of 1975: I weighed 55 kilos, was unable to sleep at night without alcoholic sedation, and had acquired an uncontrollable tremor in my hands that inconvenienced and embarrassed me in equal measure.

I retreated to Bunclody. I began to eat regularly and healthily once more, gradually recovered a regular sleeping pattern, walked the dog on a daily basis, read, watched television, listened to music, played the piano, and began to compose as soon as my hand was steady enough. With mysterious ease I wrote a piece called *Compact*, a miniature (8') concerto for piano and small orchestra, which was subsequently recorded for RTÉ by the pianist Anthony Byrne. It was quite different from earlier works, clearly showed the influences of Carter and Berio, yet possessed a degree of assured individuality. I thought of *Compact* as a small offering to those who had had faith in me: it proved that my time in Basel had not been wasted.

Chapter 16

For a time I commuted between Bunclody and Dublin, where I often stayed in the large Marlborough Road house of the artist and sculptor Eamonn O'Doherty. *Compact* seemed for the moment to have exhausted my creativity; I was at sea, and felt very ill at ease there.

That spring I applied for and won a modest Arts Council scholarship, thus ending one phase of stagnation and initiating another. I was accepted as a pupil by Mauricio Kagel, who taught music theatre in Cologne and of whom Gerald Barry had been a pupil for some time. With misgivings on all sides, I flew to Germany in October.

I moved into a flat in Adolf-Fischer-Strasse, within walking distance of the city centre. On one side of my tiny top floor room lived an English conductor who was forever singing Wagner operas to his own piano accompaniment. On the other was a professional accompanist from New Zealand, who practised diligently but at least refrained from singing. I was unfazed by this antiphony; perhaps I was placated by the hospitality of my neighbours, who occasionally invited me in for a chat and usually had a spare bottle of beer in the fridge.

I went to meet Kagel at his pleasant house in the suburbs. He asked me about my musical leanings, and my knowledge of literary and theatrical matters. Here I was in my element, and we seemed to hit it off reasonably well. He proceeded to draw two matchstick figures on a sheet of paper, within a rectangle representing the stage. He discoursed on the various possible encounters between such figures within such a space, and set me an exercise for our next lesson that entailed plotting further such intersections as exhaustively as possible.

I was disappointed that we had moved so rapidly from the discussion of ideas and history to such trivialities, as I saw them. However, I had two weeks' grace, and in the meantime resolved to put matchstick men out of my mind.

That evening a knock came to my door. It was the Romanian pianist Christian Petrescu, Stockhausen's assistant, who had heard through the grapevine that a new boy was in town. Would I be interested in studying with Stockhausen? But I was already with Kagel... That didn't matter – Stockhausen was better. But Kagel had accepted me on the basis of scores I had submitted... That didn't matter – did I have some scores I could show him, Petrescu, right now? Hmmm – yes – they seemed to be interesting pieces. OK! He'd see me on Thursday morning and introduce me to Stockhausen – cheers! And he was gone.

This whirlwind encounter filled me with conflicting emotions. I had never even considered the option of studying with Stockhausen, yet now it seemed he had come looking for me. Was this not the fulfilment of a dream? But did I really want it to be fulfilled? Was I not committed to working with Kagel, and would he not take my defection seriously amiss?

He would and did. I wrote him a note apologising profusely for my course of action and offering some lame excuses which I can no longer recall. Kagel was deeply offended, and we never spoke on the rare occasions when our paths crossed.

Whatever the rights or wrongs of my behaviour, the fact is that Kagel hated Stockhausen and Stockhausen scorned Kagel. Indeed, it was a revelation that so much mutual contempt festered between the various titans of the New Music scene. I would later marvel at the venom with which Stockhausen scoffed at Henri Pousseur's 'mindless Maoism', Boulez's 'homosexual gestures' (referring to his music, not his person), and so forth. These revelations of the pettiness of the mighty were instructive in their own way.

The following Thursday arrived after a heavily alcoholic Wednesday, and I was in bad shape when Petrescu introduced me to Stockhausen. I shamefacedly explained that I had 'come down with a stomach bug' and would not be able to sit through today's class.

'Go home and dream of me,' was his half-oracular, half-mocking injunction.

I went home via a couple of bars, where I cured my hangover and guilt feelings. Next day I was in better form, and sat through the six-hour session without incident. I was impressed that the Maestro joined us for lunch in the humble student cafeteria, although neither food nor drink passed his lips. However, not alone did he not repeat this piece of slumming, but all subsequent classes followed their lengthy course without a refreshment break.

I had brought some of my scores and had rehearsed plausible answers to imaginary questions. However, neither then nor on any subsequent occasion did Stockhausen display any interest in my work or in that of his other pupils, of whom at this stage there were only a handful.

Eventually Stockhausen concentrated his and our attentions on his most recent large-scale work, *Sirius*, which had been commissioned by the German government to celebrate the US bicentenary. This monstrosity was based mainly on four melodies from *Tierkreis*, a 1975 cycle of twelve pieces for music-boxes inspired by the signs of the Zodiac. While these miniatures were captivating and Stockhausen's analysis of them intriguing, they lost their appeal as soon as they were absorbed into the multi-layered morass of *Sirius*.

Sometimes classes were held in Stockhausen's self-designed house in Kürten, at some distance from Cologne. I found the place unnerving, in part because one was obliged to remove one's shoes and I was conscious of the less than impeccable condition of my socks. Nothing stronger than tea was on offer, of course. This added to my unease because I found it difficult to lift a teacup in my shaking hand without spilling its contents. I was always obliged to await a moment when everyone's attention was otherwise engaged, in order hastily to lift my cup in both hands and swallow down as much of the hated brew as possible.

The only classmate who shared some of my reservations about Stockhausen's teaching methods and authoritarian personality was Mike, an American. He eventually gave up composition, making him just one of several aspirant composers purged by contact with the Maestro from all desire to pursue that treacherous career.

Mike also enjoyed a beer and had a healthy interest in women. After the Stockhausen marathons we would usually embark on a pub crawl together during which, as we eyed the inaccessible female talent, he would regale me with anecdotes of his sex life 'back home'. While the point of these tales was usually self-deprecatory, I was nonetheless jealous of the unimaginable amount of rutting these extrovert Americans seemed to regard as a normal part of their daily routine.

I cannot now remember how I acquired a ticket to a concert by the Dubliners or what inspired me to avail of it. Neither can I recall how I subsequently ended up in a late night bar with several members of that celebrated folk group and their hangers-on. At one point an argument broke out between the legendary banjo player Barney McKenna and a stray shaven-headed Englishman. Barney shouted 'get your f***in' soldiers out of my f***in' country!' to which the compatriot of Shakespeare and Keats responded, 'ah, bollix!'

Soon the ancestral antagonists were rolling on the floor while barstools toppled over and beer glasses disintegrated. A minute later, the belligerents were embracing and toasting each other with the immortal phrase, 'ah sure, aren't we all human beings at the end of the day?'

Seated as I was a little apart from the fray, I caught the eye of a blond, blue-eyed woman at whom I had been staring occasionally all evening. My heart somersaulted when she joined me and introduced herself as Elfriede Schiller, telling me that she had met the musicians during a visit to Dublin. She lived in Bonn, coincidentally in Schillerstrasse, and was suitably impressed when I displayed, or simulated, some rudimentary acquaintance with the work of her illustrious literary namesake ('*Alle Menschen werden Brüder...*'). I told her that I was studying with Stockhausen and she was again suitably impressed, although of course as a leftist she disapproved of his elitism. She expressed her distaste for 'professional Irishmen' and her appreciation of the fact that I clearly wasn't one. I boldly took her hand (I was alcoholically lubricated to just the right degree) and she made no protest, but nodded in the direction of a sulky young man in denims who sat on a barstool in the midst of the revelling British Islanders, nursing a beer and staring gloomily into smoky space.

'That is my boyfriend, but we have a very open relationship.'

I took this as an invitation to kiss her, and did so enthusiastically. She laughed and drew back, shaking her head in discouragement but not rejection. Our eyes engaged in an independent dialogue, and soon we were kissing again, at great length, our hands intertwined, and I was convinced that my life was about to undergo a joyous upheaval.

'Komm, Elfriede.'

It was the importunate boyfriend. Elfriede delivered a stream of quietly vituperative German in his direction, in which I understood only the familiar and very Schillerian word *'Freiheit'* ('freedom'), and he slunk off, not before casting a murderous look in my direction.

'I'd better go,' said Elfriede, 'he gets very angry.' Had I been less intoxicated, the implication that this was a recurrent situation might have rung alarm bells. She wrote her name, address and telephone number on a beer mat, gave me a final kiss, and left.

A few days later, still in the grip of elation and a little *angeheitert* ('tipsy', but literally 'cheered up') some hours after a long Stockhausen class, I impulsively took a train the short distance to Bonn. Arriving there around 9.00 p.m., I delayed taking further action until I had seen the inside of several bars. Then I rang Elfriede who, although seeming less than enchanted by the surprise call, invited me around to her place.

I must admit that at first glance she seemed less alluring than on our first encounter, and the formality of her manner did little to improve my wilting self-assurance. Nonetheless, after a glass of wine I persuaded her to accompany me to a bar of her choice.

Thus the evening dragged on, punctuated by encounters with various friends of hers with whom she demonstratively engaged in animated conversation to my almost complete exclusion. At last, as the small hours encroached, the dreaded boyfriend and his denims materialised and led her away – but not before she had solemnly advised me not to contact her again.

This discouragement weighed heavily on me, and slotted itself all too readily into a narrative of amorous martyrdom. Again, a reasonably well-adjusted young man would heave a sigh and move on, but I lingered on this 'treachery' and brooded on the inevitability of my being 'betrayed' by every woman I 'loved'. Meanwhile, Stockhausen was turning up in the Musikhochschule less and less frequently, his classes being taken by Suzanne Stephens, his clarinet-playing companion, or by Petrescu. Furthermore, I had run out of money, and rarely had enough to eat. Eventually I was reduced to borrowing the fare for my premature return to Ireland from a friend and colleague who was himself by no means well off.

I left Cologne on a rainy March morning, carrying a heavy suitcase and a bag.

Was my period in that city a complete waste of time, and of taxpayers' money? Such questions are difficult to answer; everything that happens is grist to the mill of experience, and it is impossible to quantify the contribution of apparently barren and futile periods to outcomes that are ultimately more positive.

Of course I had heard a great deal of music in Cologne apart from Stockhausen's. The 'New Simplicity' festival had introduced me to Berio's *Coro*, Reich's *Music for 18 Musicians*, and Rzewski's *The People United will Never be Defeated*. Stockhausen was derisive about the whole concept of this festival, claiming that his vocal piece *Stimmung* (1968) had not alone anticipated the 'new simplicity' movement but also exhausted its possibilities. I obediently hated everything I heard, but it seeped into my musical subconscious nonetheless.

Admittedly, I completed not a single composition during this period. Following Stockhausen's advice I drew up a number of 'form schemes' on huge sheets of paper, using several different shades of ink. I was very proud of these visual artworks, but translated none of them into musical sounds.

In a way, my disillusionment with Stockhausen was itself a positive outcome. Eventually, I would experience it as a liberation that enabled me, when the time was ripe, to regain my own musical voice. Eventually, far in the future, I would learn to love his music all over again.

Chapter 17

Home, proverbially, is where they have to take you in. Although I never felt at home in Bunclody, it filled that role for the next eighteen months or so. My parents accepted my return with a resigned tolerance for which I gave my father some credit, and my mother none at all.

When in Dublin, I occupied a room in the Sandymount house of my university friend Dónal Hurley, who most certainly did not have to take me in but, unstintingly and to his cost, did so.

Ruminating on my misfortunes, I came to the conclusion that I was an alcoholic. Alas, this was less a revelation than a sophistry. Being an alcoholic, I could not be blamed for my actions. However, since admission of one's alcoholism was supposedly the first step towards recovery, I could drink my fill while waiting for it to happen.

My physical allergy to alcohol was such that with deadly regularity my system would break down, and I would be forced to return to Bunclody to convalesce and prepare for the next round. This probably saved me from irreparable liver damage.

I convinced myself that I drank because I was depressed, was depressed because I was lonely, and lonely because I was a sensitive genius, too shy to connect with other people, particularly women. In order to approach other people at all, I had to drink in order to overcome my inhibitions, and then my drinking frightened off other people, particularly women.

I was slim, moustached and sad-eyed, and apparently not entirely unattractive when I was not too shattered. Some women responded to my mixture of melancholy and haughtiness, but were alienated by the extent of my neediness. While desiring nothing more fervently than a long-term relationship, I dreaded the demands of commitment, one of which would clearly have been a reduction of alcohol intake. I was simultaneously addicted and allergic to a substance that perpetuated the unhappiness that in turn provided the pretext for drinking. The hell of alcoholism comprises innumerable vicious circles within a vicious circle.

Once the horrors of withdrawal had passed, my stays in Bunclody were pleasant enough – bar the occasional quarrel with my mother – and I enjoyed the sensation of health restored. I had no constant hankering after drink, although I told myself that I only endured abstention because of the prospect of ending it at a specific future date. This self-deception was part and parcel of the psychological addiction from which I could not withdraw for the simple reason that I refused to acknowledge its existence – while boasting to myself that I was clear-sighted about my alcoholism and hence not its slave.

Experts agree that resentment is a common trait of alcoholics. The drunkard's resentment is existential, free-floating, forever seeking objects on which to pin itself, and meanwhile pinning itself on what it sees – through a bottle darkly – in the mirror. The drunkard resents his or her own suffering, resenting its inevitability while simultaneously suspecting the truth: it is not inevitable at all. To fight one's way out of this tangle would, once again, mean taking responsibility for a future without alcohol. This option the drunkard resents most of all.

Why did so many people humour me in my ways, which were not alone self-destructive but often inconvenient for them? It cannot have been because I was a particularly persuasive bum: my shtick rarely strayed beyond, 'I'm broke, and really need a drink...' Perhaps some did enjoy my 'wicked evil sense of humour', as one willing victim put it prior to 'lending' me another tenner. Others may have been touched by a certain lost quality that I exuded, and believed that, since I was beyond redemption anyway, another drink could do me no harm.

ৎ　ৎ　ৎ

The German cellist Ulrich Heinen premiered my tiny new piece *Ein Blatt baumlos* at the 1978 Dublin Festival. That year's Festival Club was located in the United Arts Club, Fitzwilliam Square, where every night a succession of willing victims kept my glass filled until the small hours.

Returning to Bunclody in the bus, I was puzzled by the insistent pop music seeming to come from all corners and none. It even struck me that there were direct references to myself in the lyrics of some of the songs concerned.

Back home, I went to the bathroom and was shocked to hear the music again. I began reluctantly to accept that it was playing within my head. When I switched off the light that night and tried to sleep, the music rose to a crescendo and the words became more intelligible: they were mocking me mercilessly. Terrified as I was by this unprecedented delirium, I gradually worked out that I would have to live with it for the night. I sought somehow to distance myself from my own capricious mind, observing as dispassionately as possible the experience of hearing a quasi-demonic voice run through a repertoire of invective that I recognised as my own, to the tunes of every banal pop song of the day. By morning I had almost begun to enjoy this inner performance, and had even managed to get a few hours' sleep. By the time I rose shakily for breakfast, the demon had given up and gone silent.

ﺱ　　ﺱ　　ﺱ

In the spring of 1978 I applied for a DAAD scholarship (the acronym stands for German Academic Exchange Service) and was successful. I applied to the Korean composer Isang Yun in Berlin. He accepted me and, again full of misgivings, I prepared for my next foreign adventure.

What was I thinking of? What made me believe that this time I would make a greater success of my studies, even though nothing in my lifestyle or attitude had changed? The conviction that *this time* it would work was not all that different from the determination with which I embarked on each new binge, convinced that *this time* I would not make an ass of myself, nor incur another unbearable hangover.

Despite or because of my shortcomings, I had become involved with another woman at this point. Occasionally she would telephone me in Bunclody, after which my mother, who had never met her and knew nothing about her, would inquire 'was it that *wan* again?' Cold print cannot convey the disgust and disapproval with which she hissed out the italicised monosyllable.

This young woman probably believed that she could rescue me from myself. However, I was entirely non-cooperative in her efforts to make our relationship work, and often reduced her to tears. Simultaneously, I had become obsessed with a pretty, brown-eyed blonde, who was almost certainly bipolar and no stranger to the interior of mental hospitals. I became irrationally convinced that I, of all people, could rescue her from her demons, but she gave me no encouragement to do so and indeed treated me with a kind of benign derision.

In fleeing these entanglements, I was again seeking a geographical cure for my problems.

ڪ   ڪ   ڪ

I enrolled at the Hochschule der Künste in Berlin shortly after my arrival. My classmates were from Korea, Japan, Taiwan, Greece, the USA and Canada. The lean, curly-haired, bespectacled Canadian was named Eliot; we got into conversation, had a few beers together, and agreed to conduct a joint quest for accommodation.

We bought the *Berliner Zeitung*, a tabloid daily that had the best advertisements for flats, and drew circles around a few that seemed of interest. We took the *U-Bahn* (underground railway) to Steglitz and a double-decker bus to the nicely named suburb of Lichterfelde ('light fields') where we queued along with a half dozen others outside a house where two adjacent rooms were for rent.

I had done no serious drinking since my arrival in Berlin and was in fairly good condition. I knew that this was unlikely to last, so I was eager to take the first place that came along while I was still capable of making a good impression on a prospective landlord. The street was pleasant (a little like Griffith Avenue, I thought), the house was gracious, and the sun was shining; the disadvantages of the place were not immediately apparent. The two vacant rooms, along with a third that was already occupied and a communal kitchen and bathroom, were on the first floor and were accessed through a locked door off the landing. The rent seemed reasonable, although I would soon learn that by Berlin standards it was exorbitant. I decided to take it; Eliot was more dubious, and said he would think about it. Several days later, after I had already moved in, he did the same.

My one window overlooked Finkensteinallee, but there were trees rather than houses opposite. What nobody had told me was that Andrews Barracks was nearby, a colossal US army base from which soldiers emerged at 5.00 a.m. daily to jog up and down the street bawling the kind of slogans that Kubrick would mock in his anti-war film *Full Metal Jacket*. There was no bed, and a rather lumpy couch served as the resting place from which I daily cursed the role of US militarism in aggravating my insomnia.

My German neighbour was called Klaus. He was a few years older than myself. His family had moved from East Berlin just before the construction of the infamous Wall in 1961, but while his father had made good by embracing capitalism, Klaus had opted to remain a vague sort of communist. He was mostly unemployed, drank heavily, and spoke fluent English learned mainly from black US soldiers. Klaus and I rapidly became firm friends, despite his habit of playing rock records at maximum volume when in his cups. I soon found that the only way to cope with this was to join him, particularly as these eruptions usually meant that he had just broached a six pack or a bottle of his favourite bourbon, Jim Beam.

He lived in this confined space with two indoor cats of impressive pedigree but little personality. This necessitated keeping the window closed lest they escape; given that Klaus was a chain smoker, the atmosphere in his room could be quite fetid.

Eliot, unlike me, was irreconcilable to Klaus's music. At first he would storm down the corridor and bang loudly at his door, pleading the need to get some composing done. Often he would find me *in situ*. Then he might moderate his indignation and occasionally even join us for a beer or a whisky.

However, politeness between himself and Klaus was skin-deep at best, and relations broke down almost completely when the German cracked a supposedly 'harmless' anti-Semitic joke in Eliot's presence.

'Klaus, you do realise that I'm Jewish?' inquired Eliot very quietly, in his resonant North American bass baritone.

'My God, Eliot, I'm sorry. I swear, I didn't know...'

If anything, I was more shocked than Eliot. He appeared to expect nothing better from a German, whereas I, with some reservations, was inclined to accept Klaus's assurances. After all, he had a jocular attitude towards all peoples, including Germans, and never hesitated to make mock-disparaging remarks about the 'stupid, drunken Irish'. But of course that is not quite the same thing, given the horrors of German history.

Apart from Eliot, the only other inhabitant of the house whom I occasionally encountered was Gerd, a man whose almost total absence of teeth made it difficult to ascertain his age, but who may have been no more than forty.

One Sunday morning, while it was still dark, he knocked loudly on my door.

'They've killed Mitzi! They've killed poor little Mitzi! Come, please come!'

I pulled on some clothes and followed him apprehensively to his dark basement lair. A number of men, including Klaus, sat around a table on which a dead cat was stretched on a copy of the *Berliner Zeitung*. A trail of pinkish liquid emanated from the creature's terminally snarling mouth and stained the curves of that august journal's page three nude.

'We're having a wake for Gerd's cat,' Klaus informed me superfluously, as he poured me a glass from one of several bottles of vodka that festooned the table.

'*Verjiftet hat man se*! [She's been poisoned!]' exclaimed Gerd, pointing to the pinkish trickle, before frantically and repeatedly kissing the beast's haunches and paws and the top of her head. Mitzi continued to snarl silently.

Suspicions fell on the landlord, Herr Buhmann, who had apparently repeatedly tried to persuade Gerd to get rid of the animal.

The morning dragged on interminably. With the exception of Klaus, who was clearly enjoying himself hugely, the men had the same indeterminacy of age and scarcity of teeth as Gerd. Their Berlin dialect would have caused me sufficient difficulty had each man possessed a full set of teeth, or even dentures, so I was entirely dependent on Klaus's interpretative skills to reveal the extent of the conversation's vacuity.

Berlin was probably the last place on earth where I should have fetched up. In keeping with its anomalous status as a sealed-off capitalist enclave in the midst of the German Democratic Republic with its 'real existing socialism' (about as real as its democracy), it had a stifling atmosphere of claustrophobia. Alcoholism was endemic and seemingly universal; it was not unusual to see men in pin-striped suits, carrying expensive-looking attaché cases, barely able to walk at 3.00 or 4.00 in the afternoon.

The licensing hours were generous: bars could stay open for 23 hours daily – the 'holy hour' being between 5.00 and 6.00 a.m. when they were not allowed to serve alcohol – but could still remain open.

Klaus introduced me to Martha's Bar, nestling inconspicuously in a basement up a local side street. Its proprietor, Joe, was a huge black American ex-military policeman whose wife had reputedly spent some years in jail in her native France after killing her previous husband with a few well-aimed blows of a wine bottle. I liked her and had many half-flirtatious conversations with her, often brought to an abrupt conclusion when Joe unceremoniously ordered her to stop drinking and do this or that chore. I wondered about the future of their marriage, given the ready availability of so many bottles.

Martha's was frequented mainly by black GIs, reputedly heavily involved in drug trafficking, and German prostitutes. The latter seemed perpetually half drunk, and sported beer-bellies that significantly reduced any temptation they might have offered.

Sometimes Klaus would get part-time work on a building site and would disappear for days at a time, delivering his smelly cats to the care of one of the German prostitutes. On one such occasion I took advantage of his absence to cut down on my drinking. I closeted myself in my room – I think Eliot may already have moved out by then – and tried to read, feeling too sick and shaky to attempt work. As the late autumn evening drew in, I curled up and dozed on my couch of nails.

I woke up with a start. It was pitch dark, and loud music was coming from Klaus's room. I went out and knocked on his door, but there was no answer; the door was locked, and the music had stopped. I returned to my couch and closed my eyes, and the music recommenced. I realised that I was experiencing auditory hallucinations all over again. When I switched on the light I screamed as a buzzing creature careened towards me from the ceiling, where hordes of black moths were circling the bare lightbulb. The music had now yielded to a deafening buzzing that came from all corners of the room.

I stood up again and donned trousers and jacket. I reached for the overcoat hanging from a hook on the door, but a swarm of angry black moths that had been secreted in its folds broke cover and flew towards me. I screamed and shut my eyes tightly. Abandoning the overcoat I opened the door and, eyes still shut, propelled myself from the flat and from the house. Once on the street, inadequately dressed against the cold, I opened my eyes and rapidly made my way to Martha's, keeping as far from the shadows as possible – something was buzzing within them, but would remain at bay as long as I ignored it.

'Have you seen a ghost?' asked the barmaid.

'No, but I've seen evil black moths, which is even worse...'

'What have you been taking? Heroin? LSD?'

Truthfully, I explained that I had never taken hard drugs in my life.

'My friend,' drawled a black American army officer lounging at the bar, 'it sounds to me like you got yo'self a dose of the dee-tees! Ain't but one thing will cure that...'

And he bought me a double bourbon. And he was right.

ﺱ   ﺱ   ﺱ

I received a letter from *the wan*, suggesting that we meet soon in Paris. She was spending a few days there for purposes of work. I considered this over a few bottles of beer before writing a reply in which I claimed that I could afford neither the time nor the money to go to France. I added, unnecessarily, that this was 'probably just as well' as I felt that she would have a better time on her own. Once I had posted this, I knew that I had made a serious mistake. She was predictably hurt and angered, and wrote me another letter sharply conveying these feelings. I decided to resent her tone, and volunteered no answer.

Towards the end of November there were several days of sunlight that coincided with the impecuniousness inevitable at that time of month. One afternoon I took a long walk that led me to Zehlendorf, a leafy district in which Arnold Schoenberg had lived during one of his stays in Berlin. I was hungry but not hungover, and could appreciate the freshness and clarity of the air, and the architectural grandeur of so many of the streets through which I strolled.

I also appreciated more clearly than usual the fact that I was not living the right sort of life for a dedicated composer – and had I not decided, aged ten, that this was to be my purpose in life? I already had a few achievements under my belt, including a handful of remarkable compositions. Was I not in the process of burying this treasure instead of capitalising on it? What a contrast with the austere dedication of Schoenberg, one of my creative heroes, who might have lived and worked in one of these beautiful villas that I was admiring!

I returned home, made myself some coffee and a cheese sandwich, and resolved that from that moment on I would take full advantage of whatever Berlin offered me as a composer. I would live up to the expectations of those who had put faith in me and, just as importantly, to my own expectations.

Next day I collected my scholarship for the month of December, and my resolution disintegrated.

Chapter 18

When I returned to Berlin after spending a quiet Christmas and New Year in Ireland, I found that the great city had been hit by a winter such as I had never before experienced, with temperatures well below zero. On the first morning, I staggered to the nearest supermarket to buy provisions. Dangerously, the night's snowfall had been swept off the streets on to the footpath, where it had frozen solid. Having virtuously purchased my modest rations of cold meat, bread and chocolate biscuits, I fell flat on my face within 100 metres of home, acquiring a bloody nose and a scraped and bruised cheekbone. I knocked on Klaus's door, seeking consolation and medicine, but he was absent without leave – probably visiting his family, a bourgeois indulgence he occasionally allowed himself.

That night, clinging to the railings for support, I made my way to Martha's Bar as defiantly as a climber scaling the Eiger under adverse conditions. I was greeted like a long-lost and wounded hero by black Joe, his homicidal wife, and the whole improbable cast of waifs and strays, GIs, whores and cat-mourners.

In the small hours, well anaesthetised, I reluctantly set out for home. It was snowing, and locomotion would have been difficult even under conditions of sobriety and without the precious burden of a plastic bag containing six half-litre bottles

of beer. I had barely proceeded twenty agonisingly slow pac-
es, and was contemplating an ignominious return to the bar,
when two large policemen loomed on either side of me.

'*Ist alles in Ordnung?*' ['Is everything OK?']

Panic and paranoia swept through me. I remembered that I
had not yet got around to registering with the local authorities,
and hence did not possess a residence permit.

'*Alles in Ordnung, Danke.*'

'What happened your face?'

'I fell on the ice this morning.'

'Where are you from?'

'Dublin, Ireland.'

'What are you doing in Berlin?'

'I'm a music student at the Hochschule der Künste.'

'Do you have far to walk?'

'Just to number **, the other side of Andrews Barracks.'

'Give me your bag.'

Not alone were they about to deport me, but they were going to confiscate my beer! Sheepishly, I handed over the plastic
bag, and with a uniformed giant linking each of my arms we
trudged slowly through the snow to my door.

One policeman took my key and opened the door. His colleague carefully placed the clinking plastic bag on the hall floor.

'*Alles in Ordnung?*'

'*Ja, vielen Dank.*'

The two *Bullen* ('bulls', 'cops') saluted smartly, turned on
their heels and strolled down the Allee at a smart pace. This
was probably the most entertaining thing that had befallen
them that night, and I heard them laugh uproariously. I toast-
ed them contentedly until I drifted off to sleep.

Eliot had moved to Neukölln, a poorer area of the city were
rents were proportionately lower, and suggested that I do the

same. Simultaneously, Klaus and I were given a month's notice, Herr Buhmann having plans for renovating the building. In revenge, we took advantage of his temporary absence to raid his attic and steal a dozen bottles of homemade wine. It was revolting stuff made from sloes, blueberries or dandelions, and quite lacking in potency.

Klaus moved in with a mysterious girlfriend. Eliot helped me find new quarters in Böhmische Strasse – 'Bohemian Street' – in Neukölln – 'New Cologne'. I took these suggestive names to be a good omen. They were not.

I would now be paying a much smaller proportion of my scholarship on rent. For this I had a much larger room with its own small kitchen on the third floor. Alas, the shower and lavatory were on the landing one floor down, and possessed neither a lightbulb nor a fixture into which to insert one. Hence I tended to relieve myself in the kitchen sink, an expedient not unknown in bedsits the world over.

There was a bedstead but no mattress, so once again I contented myself with the couch.

The ceiling was high; from it there hung a single lightbulb without a shade. I lived in terror of this bulb expiring, as I had no idea how I would reach it should it need replacement.

The one large window overlooked a courtyard, or *Innenhof*, as is typical for Berlin. I was pleased that this all but excluded traffic noise, but soon found that it was used as a playground by swarms of small and very shrill children. One Saturday morning, maddened by this din, I made the mistake of opening my window and shouting '*Ruhe, bitte!*' ['Quiet, please!'] For the rest of the day the children's refrain was a jubilant '*ruabitta, ruabitta!*'

Neukölln struck me as rather a dreary district, boasting no equivalent of Martha's Bar. This was all to the good, and I soon settled into a steady routine of visiting Eliot (he lived beside the Karl-Marx-Strasse *U-Bahn* station), reading, attending lectures and trying to compose music.

During my Christmas stay in Dublin I had in fact secured a modest commission from the young flautist Derek Moore. I drafted *Mutatis mutandis* in Bunclody, and now set about producing a definitive version. Although he eventually paid me for it, Derek did not like the piece, which entailed some rather clownish theatricals, and never played it. Sadly, a few short years later he would die of AIDS in Amsterdam, the first acquaintance of mine to suffer this fate. He was a terrific player, and a great loss to Irish musical life.

Emboldened by the completion of a new work, however short, I made the absurd decision to embark on nothing less than a full-length opera. I had long been fascinated by *Melmoth the Wanderer*, a labyrinthine 1820 gothic novel by the Dubliner Charles Maturin. Try as I might, I could envisage no adaptation that did not in some way straighten out its convolutions, thus doing unacceptable violence to it.

Next, I turned to Berthold Brecht's early expressionist play *Im Dickicht der Städte* (literally, *In the Thicket of Cities*). Here, too, abridgement would have been necessary but it seemed to me that the essence of the play could be retained.

In the event, although I drafted libretto after libretto, I committed no music to paper. Still, the hours spent mulling over these abortive projects were scarcely wasted; they brought me face to face with important stylistic issues and kept me temporarily off the streets.

Then Klaus turned up on my doorstep. The mysterious girlfriend had thrown him out, he had given away his cats for good, and was in need of temporary accommodation.

As my relatively industrious solitude was becoming burdensome, I readily acquiesced in this arrangement. Klaus would sleep on the spare bed, and was unfazed by the absence of a mattress. The bedstead, in classic German fashion, was constructed with chains secured by springs, a little like a trampoline. Klaus tossed and turned continuously in his sleep, thus causing a loud jangling noise that woke me up repeatedly or prevented me from falling asleep.

In return for my hospitality, Klaus offered to cook. I had grisly memories of his preparing *Eisbein* in Lichterfelde, admittedly for his own exclusive consumption – boiled pickled ham-hock, heavily marbled and covered with a thick layer of fat – a kind of gastronomic equivalent of *Schlager*, those unspeakable German pop songs that can only be endured in a spirit of postmodern irony and/or inebriation. He reassured me that he had nothing so meaty in mind, and cooked what he called *spaghetti carbonara,* pasta with a raw egg thrown in and plenty of black pepper on top. This rudimentary dish was easy to eat, and lined the stomach satisfactorily for the more important business of drinking.

One afternoon Klaus arrived back with some extra money and suggested we go shopping. We visited a local supermarket and stocked up on food and beer, for which he insisted on paying. Back on the street and barely out of visibility of the store, he whipped open his bulky overcoat to reveal an entire drinks cabinet illicitly stashed in a plethora of reinforced pockets clearly sown in place for such a purpose: bottles of brandy, bourbon, gin, vodka and Armagnac. For several days and nights I took leave of reality; the inevitable aftermath was a week of prostration and acute guilt feelings.

Eliot took a dim view of Klaus's re-entry into my life, with its attendant effects on my concentration and my attendance at Yun's classes. Klaus in turn regarded Eliot as a snob and resented the Canadian's lingering belief in his anti-Semitism, a vice which he stoutly denied.

No sooner had I picked myself up from this bout than I was obliged to attend an interview in Bonn to determine whether my scholarship should be renewed. I had submitted the flute-piece, a new version of *Embers*, and a third piece nostalgically called *Light-Fields*, which I cobbled together from various exercises I had composed for Yun. I was now confronted by a solemn panel of the great and good (the Swiss composer Klaus Huber is the only one I remember) who interrogated me concerning my compositional procedures and future plans.

I had had just enough drink prior to this ordeal to ease my nerves and loosen my tongue. I emerged feeling that I had not made a complete fool of myself, although I proceeded to do so on the train back to Berlin (I was saving the German government's money by not taking a return flight) when I fell asleep in the dining car and, awakened by an inspector, was unable for some time to find the compartment where I had cleverly left my ticket.

ک   ک   ک

Patricia had decided to take a trip to New York, and had invited me to come along. She had posted the tickets to me, including one for a flight to Paris where we were to meet. All that remained was for me to visit the US Consulate and procure a visa.

The prospect of this trip dismayed me. In the wake of my kleptomaniac binge with Klaus I had again lost control of my drinking. I was terrified of failing to link up with Patricia at Charles de Gaulle Airport. I dreaded the long, claustrophobic flight over the Atlantic. I was intimidated by the thought of

New York City, with its vertiginous skyscrapers, its aggressive Irish-American cops, and its over-expensive alcohol. But most of all I dreaded visiting the US Consulate, and kept postponing the evil day.

Meantime Klaus, to whom I had mentioned my past attachment to a singer called Chi Coltrane, noticed that she was due to perform in Berlin and somehow secured us two tickets. The venue was an enormous indoor stadium, and although we arrived long before Coltrane was due on stage, the place was suffocatingly full. We secured standing places at the back, reassuringly close to the bar.

By the time Coltrane appeared, I had endured a succession of German *Schlager*-singers and had washed them down with too much beer. I could barely distinguish the faraway blond singer's frame, the sound system conveyed a distorted version of her distinctive voice, and the Berliners milling in our vicinity clearly had no interest in her and were drowning her out with their raucous bellowing.

After this fiasco, as we made our way back to Böhmische Strasse via a couple of the unsavoury local pubs, I was beginning to feel increasingly weak and dizzy. Scarcely had we reached the front door when everything went black and I fell over, striking my head on the pavement and cutting open my forehead. Klaus somehow managed to resuscitate me, help me upstairs, wash my wound and put me to bed.

The deadline for seeking a US visa being upon me, I had no choice but to drag myself to the US consulate a couple of days later. The polite and solicitous official, confronted with this shaking, ill-shaven and recently scarred young man, unsurprisingly informed me that 'this time' I was clearly in no condition to avail of a visa, but that I should 'look after myself' and visit the USA at some future date.

Of course I should have telephoned my sister and informed her that I would not be travelling. I should have immediately posted the tickets back to her so that she could secure a refund. But I was in denial at what had happened; irrationally, I convinced myself that in a few days I would be better, the evidence of my accident would have vanished, and the Americans would change their minds and grant me a visa.

The days passed, and I looked and felt just as bad. Unable to contemplate making a long-distance telephone call (there was no telephone in the flat), I wrote to Patricia explaining what had happened, but without returning the tickets (I would eventually get a partial refund for them in Dublin, which bought me a few drinks). By now it was too late and my letter did not reach her in time. She waited vainly at Charles de Gaulle and boarded the transatlantic flight in a state of frantic worry.

I went to the Hochschule and asked the Secretary whether my scholarship had perhaps been renewed. She informed me that she had no news, but that the DAAD was under financial pressure and was renewing very few scholarships for students in Berlin, 'particularly composition students', she added with what I interpreted as hostile emphasis.

I called on Eliot and, in bridge-burning mood, quarrelled with him about I know not what. I returned to Böhmische Strasse and quarrelled with Klaus, blaming him for my bruised face, my failure to obtain a visa, my inability to sleep at night, and my excessive drinking. He defended himself emotionally, packed a bag and left. I threw myself on the couch, pulled the sleeping bag over my head, and drew up an inventory of my existence: I had lost my friends, my sister, my creative gifts, my scholarship and my health. I was scraped clean, and had never felt so dirty.

That night I went on a pub crawl along the Sonnenallee, a long street where the bars were anonymous and unpretentious. I was seeking adventure, by which I meant female companionship. In a large barn-like *Kneipe*, particularly attractive to me because so many of its clients were asleep with their heads on their folded arms, I got into conversation with a Polish immigrant who was soon returning to his native country. He had never heard of Lutoslawski or Penderecki, Bruno Schulz or Gombrowicz, Polanski or Wajda, but he insisted on buying me several Polish vodkas, and struck me as an all-round good fellow – but this was no adventure.

In the subsequent bars that I visited, I read a book called *The Manufacture of Madness*, failed to get properly drunk, and had no adventures.

Next evening I went by train to the Wannsee, a region and lake in southwest Berlin, and looked for the place where the dramatist Heinrich von Kleist had committed suicide in 1811 and subsequently been buried. I made inquiries of a variety of solid citizens, but not one of them had ever heard of Heinrich von Kleist. I had no adventures, suffered no disasters, and again failed to get properly drunk.

Next day was Friday the thirteenth. I rose early, feeling physically quite well, and shaking only moderately. Normally on a Friday I would go to the local Berliner Bank, collect a payment slip, and either take it to a local bar or back home to fill out and sign. Today I was so steady that I could probably have executed this manoeuvre before a cashier without falling to pieces. Instead, I counted my change and calculated that I could visit three bars and have two small beers in each. This would provide three final opportunities for adventure.

I first went to a *Kneipe* on the corner of Karl-Marx-Strasse where I had once or twice played cards with Klaus. The place was empty, and remained so although I sipped my quota of beer very slowly.

The second bar was closer to home and a little livelier, but its clientele was exclusively male. There were no adventures to be had.

For my third and final attempt I went upmarket, visiting a square in the vicinity that was architecturally less unprepossessing than the rest of Neukölln. There were two bars to choose from; the one I selected even boasted an attractive waitress, but was otherwise unpromising. Lunchtime was upon us, and the place rapidly filled up with businessmen and -women, ordering food and engaging in business-like conversation. The waitress seemed barely able to keep pace with their orders.

It took some time for me to attract her attention and order my second drink, which she slapped in front of me without ceremony. This, then, was a very special drink. I thought of it as an hourglass, and after the first sip held it up to the light, measuring what remained of the future.

There was no going back, and no desire to go back. Soon only a mouthful remained in the glass, and there were to be no more adventures save one, and that one would take place in solitude. I drank up, paid, and left.

I walked home slowly, my head clear, my mind calm. Outside my front door I inspected the pavement and confirmed to my own satisfaction that my personal bloodstain was still in evidence. I had left a mark on Berlin!

Back in the flat I washed the dishes, dried the bottom of the green plastic basin that had contained them, brought it into the living room, and set it down on the floor beside my couch.

I removed the blade from my razor; it was a little rusty, but that scarcely mattered now.

I lay on the couch, wearing t-shirt and jeans. I held my left wrist over the basin and drew the blade across it. To my surprise, blood spouted in all directions except into the basin. The pain was acute, but rapidly diminished. I let the wound drip for a while before transferring the blade to my left thumb and index finger and slicing my right wrist. This time there was no gush of blood. Indeed, for a moment it seemed as if I must try again, but then a thin line of blood formed and began to trickle. I positioned myself as comfortably as I could on the hard couch, both wrists dripping peacefully into the green plastic basin. I closed my eyes and waited. I cannot say that the events of my life passed in rapid procession before my drowning inner eye. I cannot even say that self-pity was what I felt, although it certainly tinged the dominant emotion: a passionless, exhausted and impersonal resentment as darkness fell.

ڪ   ڪ   ڪ

'You stupid, mad Irishman, what have you done! You stupid, mad Irishman, wake up!'

I was being shaken and my cheeks were being slapped by Klaus, whose eyes were wet with tears. He had come back to collect the remainder of his personal possessions and return the key of the flat, and had found me unconscious, my wrists suspended limply above the green plastic basin, now stained with brackish blood.

As a conscientious objector Klaus had chosen to undergo training as a male nurse instead of performing military service (compulsory in Germany until 2011) or going to jail. He now tore up a tea towel and bandaged my wrists provisionally, before running to a nearby pharmacy and buying bandages, ointment and some kind of antiseptic powder. He washed and dressed the wounds properly, muttering imprecations about 'crazy Irishmen' as he worked. Then he ran out and bought a six-pack of beer, and I proceeded to build myself up again.

Not alone was the wallpaper above the couch spattered with blood from my left wrist, but even the ceiling had been daubed. I gazed placidly at the irregular scarlet patterns, feeling a little dreamy and resigned to the fact that my Berlin days, like so many days before them, had ended in defeat. As I meditatively drank my beer, nothing was further from my mind than the idea of ending it all. It was as if, temporarily at any rate, I had drained the depression from myself with the several pints of blood that I had lost.

For a few days I remained obediently on the couch while Klaus fed and watered me, and dressed my wounds. My un-canny recuperative powers having kicked in, I was eager to be up and about and preparing my departure from Berlin. Klaus warned me to cover the bandages with my sleeves despite the hot summer weather, since suicide was still a crime in Ger-many and, strictly speaking, he should have reported me to the authorities. I visited Eliot and was reconciled, and perhaps it was not without a certain perverse pride that I recounted my harrowing adventure. He called around to the flat and helped Klaus clean blood from the ceiling. Thus, after all, even these two had been to some degree reconciled.

And now, irony of ironies, I received a letter from the Hoch-schule. The DAAD, not having been informed of my change of address, had mistakenly posted to Lichterfelde the news that my scholarship had been renewed. I was to be congratulated on this achievement, and it was to be hoped that I would spend a successful second year in Berlin!

This was not an option. I passed on the Böhmische Strasse flat to Klaus, and returned to Ireland.

Chapter 19

I hung around Dublin for several weeks in the hope that the scars on my wrists would be less conspicuous by the time I visited my parents. This did not mean that, once a few drinks had loosened my inhibitions, I was shy of displaying them as testimony to my life of sensitive martyrdom.

One afternoon a 21-year-old German woman called Renate was introduced to me in Bewley's famous Grafton Street coffee shop during the 'holy hour' between 14.30 and 15.30. On learning her nationality, not readily apparent from her fluent English, I brandished my wounds and explained how I had acquired them. If this was intended as a gambit of seduction, it failed miserably. She was 'not impressed', and roundly told me so. I decided there and then that she was a stuck-up prig.

In late 1979 I drifted into an intense but unconsummated liaison with a married woman. It was clear to both of us that nothing could come of this relationship, yet it limped along wretchedly for months. Eventually, exhausted, ravaged and yearning to become a completely different person, I committed myself to St Brendan's Mental Hospital, Grangegorman.

This also proved a dead end. I was sedated and fed, and left to my own devices. Nobody came to talk to me or suggest any programme of rehabilitation. Occasionally a hefty young man injected me in the backside with sadistic glee. After five days, scarcely able to walk, I discharged myself and made a bee-line for Kehoe's pub in South Anne Street. I would remain the same person for a while longer.

Despite this turmoil, music began to trickle from me again. I composed *Aprèslude* for the Concorde Ensemble, who premiered it in the January 1980 Dublin Festival. I followed this up, unsolicited, with *Tristia* for soprano and ensemble. I set out to make these three settings of poems by Dickinson, Celan and Thomas Hardy the saddest songs ever composed, but some imp of the perverse induced me to add a purely instrumental postlude tentatively intruding a note almost bordering on hope, an emotion I was not conscious of feeling but that must have lurked somewhere under the ice.

I won the Macaulay Fellowship which 'is made to further the liberal education of a young creative artist, and can be used for any purpose that facilitates this aim'. This in turn was followed by a commission from the Performing Right Society (PRS) to compose a large-scale piece to inaugurate the grand piano that would be installed in Dublin's National Concert Hall, then still under construction.

In early 1981, I travelled to Brittany with a friend, John C. At the tourist office in Roscoff I rented an apartment overlooking the Atlantic and the island of Batz, which instantly became a location of fantasy comparable to the Ballycroy of my childhood. John took the bedroom, and I camped on the couch in the living room, force of habit reasserting itself.

John stocked up with food and I stockpiled alcohol. I set to work on my new Sonata, once again attempting to prove to myself that I did not need a piano to compose. The weather was mostly grim, and a baleful foghorn punctuated the windswept silence with oppressive regularity.

Nothing came to me. John cooked gargantuan stews that lasted for several days at a time. I usually left the consumption of this nourishing fare to him, while I visited a local bar, played Alain Stivell on the jukebox, drank beer, and returned with a six-pack clutched possessively in each hand.

We watched TV. On 23 February, Lt. Col Antonio Tejero Molina of the Guardia Civil stormed into the Spanish parliament with 200 armed men. A film called *The Cassandra Crossing*, dubbed in French, dealt with the outbreak of a deadly disease on a train. I found both spectacles entirely incomprehensible.

The foghorn added its doleful commentary.

I soon realised that I would make no progress with my Sonata. To prove that I had tried, I collected my stray sketches and posted them to the composer James Wilson, who was representing the PRS in the matter of this commission. I enclosed a cheque for the share of the fee I had already been paid, explaining that I was too ill to complete the piece to schedule. Within a few days, Wilson had returned the cheque and sketches, with the news that the concert had been postponed. I had time to recover and complete the piece, and he wished me the best of luck.

John cooked and ate his stews, I drank beer and wine, sometimes at home and sometimes in a bar where dour fisherman looked askance at me as I listened to Alain Stivell and read Jean Cayrol's gloomy novel *Je vivrai l'amour des autres*. I watched television listlessly, my eyes burning.

The weather improved, and John suggested we walk to the nearby village of Saint-Pol-de-Léon. The sun shone and birds sang as we set out along the coast. It was cool, but spring was probably not too far off. I looked across the fields, and was distracted by a black speck hovering in the sky, perhaps a bird of prey. It instilled a vague unease in me that rapidly turned to panic as it started buzzing threateningly. Then it careened towards me, acquiring amplitude and a flaming orange nimbus as the buzzing increased in volume. I screamed, threw out my arms to fend it off, and collapsed unconscious.

'My God, you put the heart crosswise on me,' said John, leaning over me solicitously as I lay in the middle of the narrow road, the ocean whispering to my left.

'Where are we?' I asked, looking around at the sunny, unfamiliar landscape.

'Are you serious? We're in Brittany, about a mile outside Roscoff.'

He helped me to my feet, and as we made our way back to the town I slowly reconstructed my identity and my environment.

It appeared that I had only been unconscious for a few moments. When John opined that this was some kind of epileptic fit, I was struck with horror: had this bogey from my childhood pursued me to Brittany and finally caught up with me? As for John, he had had enough of this madness. Next day he stocked the larder with food and apologetically set out to hitchhike to Bavaria, where a woman was waiting for him.

I was now afraid to leave the apartment lest I be assaulted by flying horrors while walking the streets, or sitting in a bar. The weather deteriorated, and my hours were again punctuated by that lugubrious foghorn. I had polished off all the alcohol in the house except for a small bottle of Armagnac, for which I had little taste. I had no appetite, and was unable to concentrate on Cayrol or the most trivial TV programmes.

A single large tomato sat on a plate in the middle of the dining table. It had acquired a cap of blue mould, and I acknowledged that at some point I would have to bestir myself and throw it out, a prospect that I found peculiarly terrifying. I stared at it, wondering if perhaps I could cut it in half and eat the unblemished part. It stared back at me, and began to buzz.

Suddenly it took off from its plate and spun through the air, buzzing with fierce malignity. I shouted and thrust out an arm to deflect it.

I came to myself lying on the floor, and once again had difficulty identifying my environment. The rotting tomato sat innocently on its plate. A gale howled outside, and the foghorn moaned through the gale. I dragged myself to the couch, pulled the mound of bedclothes over my shivering frame, and drank the remainder of the Armagnac in a long gulp. I fell into an uneasy doze.

When I awoke I was standing in an arched room atop the spire of Findlater's Church in Dublin's Parnell Square. At the other end of the room sat a man in clerical garb. Somehow I knew him to be a Dominican and an inquisitor. I noted with revulsion that the top of his skull was missing, and knew that if I stood on tiptoe I would be able to see the buzzing, fermenting mess in his brain-pan.

'My son,' he murmured, 'you know perfectly well what you are guilty of. Much though I regret it, I must ensure that you undergo a fitting punishment.'

He waved his left hand, and a door beside him opened. For a moment nothing happened, then something slithered through the aperture, followed by another slithering something. Soon a whole brood of snakes was undulating into the room in my direction. Worse still: they were not intact. Each serpent had been neatly cut in two, and from its pinkish, slightly frothing flesh tiny blobs fell to the floor and started to grow into new half-snakes that writhed purposefully towards me.

I screamed as loud and often as I could. An urgent knock came to the door. Aware both that I was in an apartment in

Roscoff and that I was about to be rescued from the Inquisition in Dublin, I struggled from my couch and unlocked the door.

It was my Uncle Jack from Bournemouth, with whom I had unfinished business.

'What right did you have to slap my dog Rebel on the snout?' I shouted.

'*Ce n'est pas le ton*' ['That's not the right tone'], he replied reproachfully. Why was he speaking in French?

Somehow he coaxed me back on the couch. He picked up the telephone which I had never used, and spoke quietly, still in French. Soon somebody rang the front doorbell, and nice M. Gascoigne from the tourist office, whom I still identified as my Uncle Jack, politely and gently escorted me down to the waiting ambulance.

I was driven to the Centre Hospitalier in Morlaix, a large town some twelve miles from Roscoff. I was puzzled that this journey took me through the familiar boglands of Achill Island, a puzzlement I conveyed in English to the white-robed male nurse who sat beside me. He was even more puzzled.

On arrival I was stripped, clad in hospital pyjamas, and put to bed. As I showed some inclination to get up again immediately, I was strapped down and given an injection. As I lay there, gazing at the white ceiling, I noticed appreciatively that it was covered with ants. These were no ordinary termites: they were performing a spectacular ballet, moving in complex formations to the *pizzicato* Scherzo from Bartok's *Fourth String Quartet*. This vivid phantasmagoria was interrupted by a deep, dreamless sleep.

I awoke the next day in a lucid state, and with a healthy appetite for breakfast. Shortly thereafter I was visited by a stern but not unfriendly doctor who, in answer to my anxious query, assured me that there was no question of my leaving before at least a week was out.

A nurse set up a drip, into which three times daily for the next two days she injected a substance that hurt agonisingly as it entered my system. The stern but kindly doctor visited me, performed various tests, and informed me that M. Gascoigne had been asking after my welfare, and had guaranteed that I would be welcome to return to the flat when I was better.

After a week of this, I was released. The doctor told me the bill would be forwarded to my parents, whose address I had provided. From now on, he admonished me, I was to drink nothing stronger than water – not even coffee.

I took a taxi to the station, bought a ticket for Roscoff, and settled down in the bar with a newspaper. After a moment's hesitation, I ordered a beer; it tasted delicious.

M. Gascoigne helped me book my passage back to Ireland on a ferry leaving for Cork two days hence, and I duly paid him the rent he was owed. He saw me off at the ferry, seeming baffled by my apparent good health and perturbed by my drinking a parting glass of beer. He was such a nice man that he seemed reluctant to see me go, although he can rarely have had a more worrying tenant.

On arrival in Ireland, I sensibly went straight to Bunclody and got back to work on my abandoned Sonata, finishing it ahead of deadline several weeks later. I racked my brain for an explanation for the bill from Morlaix, the imminent arrival of which I nervously anticipated. However, either it never arrived, or my parents discreetly chose not to mention it, perhaps dreading any explanation I might offer.

On 12 September John O'Conor, at that time Ireland's leading concert pianist, gave the first performance of my second *Piano Sonata*. I sat in the VIP gallery of the new National

Concert Hall. On my left sat James Wilson and Howard Ferguson, a venerable composer from Northern Ireland, while on my right sat Mick L., one of my most rakish drinking buddies. Mick and I had smuggled two bottles of ale into the hall, from which we sipped indiscreetly as John played; I brandished mine in a salute to John O'Conor and the audience when I took my bow.

Afterwards I posed for the press alongside O'Conor. In one photograph the pianist looks resigned and composed, the composer deranged and discomposed. And yet the Sonata itself is an austere, highly formal work that betrays not a hint of the psychological thicket from which it emerged.

A few days later I went to Annaghmakerrig House, an 'artists' retreat' near the small but beautifully named town of Newbliss just south of the border in County Monaghan. Although the Centre had yet to be officially opened, several artists had been invited to try the place out in advance.

The Centre's director was Bernard Loughlin, a Belfast man who appeared to take a sharply mordant view on people and things, and of whom I was at first a little wary. The house was a stately Victorian pile overlooking a lake and surrounded by woods and the drumlins (small hills of glacial origin) so characteristic of the landscape in Counties Cavan and Monaghan. I was housed in a large bedroom that would later be dubbed the John Jordan Room, after the writer and critic. It had an en-suite bathroom and an open fireplace.

During this first visit, the room next door to mine was inhabited by Gerald Barry. I greatly appreciated his willingness to light the fire in my room, an art I had never mastered, and at which he was skilled. Most nights I would sit in an armchair in the glow and warmth of that fire, drinking hot whiskey and reading *The Count of Monte Cristo* or *Martin Chuzzlewit*. On other occasions Gerald would knock on my door after mid-night and we would walk in the woods by the big house. Once we strolled through the wintry forest at 3.00 a.m., moonlight on the snow creating an effect of daylight. We entered a clearing and were confronted by a herd of deer that stood motionless as a ghostly army for what seemed like several minutes before unanimously erupting into motion and disappearing noisily into the undergrowth.

Although my first stay at Annaghmakerrig was punctuated by binges with subsequent torments of withdrawal, all the more humiliating for taking place in a semi-public environment, it was all in all a time of sociability and industry.

Among the other inmates of the Centre were the journalist and civil rights activist Nell McCafferty, the playwright M.J. Molloy, the (eventually) very successful novelist Colm Tóibín, in those days long-haired and sulky, and the above-mentioned John Jordan for whom I developed a great affection not un-linked to the 'mind for a dhrop' that had on occasion led to his admission to St. Patrick's Hospital.

One night Gerald Barry and I gave a piano duet recital for the resident artists in which we included several sections from Ravel's exquisite *Mother Goose Suite*. During the few years that remained to him, John Jordan never failed to rhapsodise about this performance whenever I met him.

In the course of one party, just before the Centre closed for Christmas, several resident artists recited and sang party pieces while John sat slumped in his chair in the state of stupor to which it took less and less liquor to reduce him. During a lull in the revels, he suddenly raised his head, commanded silence, and recited – word perfect – Patrick Kavanagh's 'Raglan Road':

On Raglan Road on an autumn day I met
her first and knew
That her dark hair would weave a snare
that I might one day rue;
I saw the danger, yet I walked along the
enchanted way,
And I said, let grief be a fallen leaf at the
dawning of the day.

There was a sadness in his voice and a remoteness in his gaze that made this moving performance something transcending a mere party piece, something suggestive of mournful experiences beyond the ken of anyone else in the room. Once he had finished and his head had sunk once more on his chest, applause was followed by a chastened silence, and we all retired to bed.

In Annaghmakerrig I worked, and worked hard. I had secured a large quantity of 36-stave orchestral manuscript paper and resolved to fulfil my childhood dream of composing a piece for an orchestra of cineramic dimensions. The result was *Enchaînement*, a 17' piece most of which I composed in fair copy during those long, dark days. It is a piece of considerable formal rigour based on seven interrelated melodies. An orchestra of over 100 players is only occasionally used for mass effect. *Enchaînement* is an exuberant and hectic piece, and its composition – which I finished in Bunclody over Christmas and the New Year – was an unexpectedly joyous experience. Clearly all was not lost!

Chapter 20

I started writing concert reviews for *Soundpost*, a music journal edited by Michael Dervan. This naturally entailed attending concerts, something that I usually avoided unless they included music by myself.

Dervan offered me a regular back page column in *Soundpost*, to be rather cleverly called 'Tailpiece'. For six months I wrote polemical and dogmatic articles that annoyed a great many people, amused some, and brought me in a small but welcome income,

Early in 1983 I felt sufficiently confident to move into a bedsit on my own. This was in Dufferin Avenue off the South Circular Road, not far from the National Stadium where I had attended *Messiah* on the evening I had learned of my father's drinking. I had a small room in the back of the house overlooking the playground of a primary school; I found that the noise of children playing at predictable times for short periods was pleasant rather than troublesome, and not comparable to the Berlin children's '*ruabitta!*' I retrieved the Ferguson record player and my records from Bunclody, and joined Kevin Street public library which in those days housed the Music Library. I went on the dole and signed up for rent allowance, which was supplemented by an allowance of butter, not to be despised.

Once a week, on dole day, I would buy a stock of potatoes, onions, carrots, tomatoes, parsnips and minced beef, and cook a hefty stew in the manner of John C. This would line my stomach for the evening's drinking, which took place either in a city centre pub in the company of a small circle of dedicated time-wasters, or in solitude in one of the featureless local establishments. I spent my thirtieth birthday on a solitary pub crawl in the region of Portobello, ending up in a republican haunt where bearded musicians sang patriotic songs and I joined in as raucously as I could. I took a taxi home, feeling maudlin but not too unhappy.

When money ran out I would sit at home, listen to music and read. The electricity was governed by a meter into which one fed fifty-pence pieces. The winter had been exceptionally chilly and early spring was not much better. The bedsit was anything but warm, but the electric fire devoured current. I would sit in my armchair wearing an overcoat, the quilt from my bed draped over me, and a hot water bottle cradled on my knees. Nonetheless, on more than one occasion my reading was interrupted by a loud click followed by frustrating darkness. On such occasions, if it was too early for bed, I would walk to the city centre looking for friends who, if they could not afford to buy me a few drinks, might 'lend' me the wherewithal to return home and feed the merciless meter.

At that time *In Dublin* magazine, published by John S. Doyle and edited by David McKenna, was a respected outlet for reviews and features of a liberal-to-leftist persuasion. I asked McKenna if I could write occasional articles about music, but to my surprise and discomfort he offered me the post of theatre critic that had recently been vacated by Fintan O'Toole. To refuse would have been to look a gift horse in the mouth. To accept would have been to enter waters where, I feared, I was out of my depth. I conveyed this anxiety to McKenna, but he claimed that an outsider's perspective was precisely what he was seeking. I accepted, and my life took another twist.

On 20 April I went for a drink to The Bailey in Duke Street, at that time a meeting place favoured by those with bohemian pretentions and reputedly a good place for meeting women. And indeed as soon as I entered I noticed one, who happened to be seated with my friend John C. (Dublin is a small city). I bought drinks for them and, probably to John's annoyance, sat at their table.

The young woman's name was Anette, she was German, had curly reddish-blond hair and the largest pair of brown eyes I had ever seen. I talked about my new job as a theatre critic, and mentioned that I would be seeing *Hamlet* in the Abbey Theatre the following Friday. Anette expressed her enthusiasm for the play, I invited her to accompany me, she accepted, and my life's new twist took another turn.

We met an hour before the play in The Crowing Cock, a pub opposite the theatre. She drank vodka and lime, I drank beer, and we were soon reasonably at ease together. During the interval and in the pub afterwards, Anette's comments were articulate and to the point. We made a date for the following Tuesday and separated with a kiss. I lay awake much of that night reliving and interpreting that kiss. How intimate had it really been? How much promise had it really contained?

On Tuesday we got drunk together. After closing time we went to a horrible nightclub called McGonagle's in South Anne Street, where we drank an appreciable quantity of disagreeable rot-gut wine. Afterwards she spent the night with me in my narrow bed with its musty sheets. We were tipsy and tired, and next morning we both felt the worse for wear and had little to say to each other. We went our separate ways, having pledged to meet in Bewley's that afternoon. Disconsolate, convinced that I had seen the last of her, I turned up ahead of schedule – and there she was!

From then on she accompanied me to most of the plays I was obliged to review, frequently suggesting the line I might take in my article, and occasionally all but writing it herself when over-indulgence had dulled my memory. After the shows, we would usually go back to her place in Sandymount, and would often drink a nightcap in Ryan's pub on Sandymount Green. Although she was disapproving when I set out the next morning to top up with the hair of the dog, by and large harmony reigned.

RTÉ commissioned me to compose the station's entry for the following year's Italia Prize for radiophonic works. I resolved to write a kind of radio opera in homage to one of my favourite authors, E.T.A. Hoffmann. This would simultaneously be a kind of postmodern homage to the nineteenth century itself. I would base it on Hoffmann's story *Rat Krespel*, which is also the basis of the second act of Offenbach's *Tales of Hoffmann*.

The first instalment of my commission fee enabled me to fly with Anette to meet her parents in the village of Buer in North-Rhein Westphalia. For me, of course, this was a major ordeal, and I am sure the retired watchmaker and his amiable wife had no idea what to make of me. Ill-at-ease, I availed of a lift to Berlin, where Eliot still lived and was working as an English teacher. I drank too much, and returned to Buer in a rather shattered state. This can hardly have convinced my hosts that their daughter had made a wise choice, and Anette herself must have had nagging doubts.

Shortly after we returned to Dublin she moved into a flat nearer the city. When that proved unsuitable, I was able to persuade her against her better judgment that we should move together into a top-storey flat on the corner of Adelaide Road and Earlsfort Terrace, site of the National Concert Hall.

I loved this small flat for its location and its altitude, despite the considerable traffic noise that rose from the junction of two busy streets. I loved it mainly, however, because it represented my first attempt at cohabitation and hence seemed to symbolise my emergence from solitude, a condition that I had come to experience as shameful, even somehow reprehensible.

Anette was less confident. It was here that the pattern of our affectionate and quarrelsome coexistence would be established, only to be shattered after a few weeks when Anette was notified that she would be obliged to return to Germany in the autumn. She had been awarded a teaching traineeship (*Referendariat*) in the northwestern city of Oldenburg.

This struck me as a blow of fate maliciously directed at myself! I had at last begun to set my life in order, and felt that I had been justly rewarded. This was now to be plucked from my grasp, and in addition I would not be able to afford to maintain the Adelaide Road refuge. I suggested with some temerity that Anette should consider rejecting or at least postponing acceptance of the German state's offer. Realising that I was distraught, but rightly determined on not letting this opportunity pass, she tentatively and with obvious reluctance suggested that I should accompany her to Oldenburg. At that point the idea seemed as impossible to myself as it did to her, and it was dropped. As the weeks passed, however, I realised that for once I could not yield to my fatalism – come hell or high water I would also move to Oldenburg! Anette was profoundly uncomfortable at this prospect but, somewhat to my own surprise, I persuaded her to consent to the idea. Perhaps she was not convinced that I had it in me to make such a drastic move.

Now the Dublin Theatre Festival started and I was committed to attending upwards of twenty productions. Meanwhile, Anette's parents arrived in town. After a brief holiday during which they visited the usual sights, they whisked her away from me.

I was at best an erratic theatre critic. Imbued as I was with an antipathy to realism and anything smacking of the kitchen sink, I would have been content with a diet of Genet, Pinter, Beckett and Gombrowicz. Failing that, I enjoyed traditionalist productions of Shakespeare and scorned productions of a Marxist bent that sought to imbue classic works with 'relevance', which I equated with topicality and considered an insult to the audience's capacity for imaginative projection. I dismissed most recent Irish plays as lacking in modernism, and falling pathetically short of the most radical traditions of Irish writing. These stances once or twice almost led to blows with writers and actors who frequented the same bars as I did. Certainly such views conflicted dramatically with those of *In Dublin*'s editor, and it is to his credit that he never attempted to rein me in or censor my reviews.

I attended the last few Festival events on my own, devastated, usually less than entirely sober, and frequently leaving during the interval. I moved out of Adelaide Road, staying for a few nights in the York Street flat of the writer Leland Bardwell, a famously hospitable woman whom I had met in Annaghmakerrig. On the day after the Festival had finished I used her battered typewriter – and a naggin of whiskey – to type up my notes for *In Dublin*. I then moved back to Bunclody for two months where I completed work on *Krespel*, a 30' piece for soloists, chorus and orchestra.

On balance, the two and a half years since my crisis in Brittany had seen me pick myself off the ground and embark on a stumbling process of rehabilitation. I still drank too much, and my hangovers were getting worse. Nonetheless, I had been musically productive, had started writing regularly on musical and theatrical matters, and had even held down a job of sorts for half a year. Most remarkably, I had embarked on a promising relationship with a captivating and intelligent woman. I had persuaded her to live with me in Dublin and agree to my joining her in Germany. I had earned money and, unprecedentedly, had even managed to save some of it. Like Don Quixote picking himself up and remounting Rosinante, I set out for Germany imbued with feelings of confidence and optimism that were entirely new to me.

Chapter 21

Located fifty kilometres from the North Sea, Oldenburg is a prosperous city that in 1983 had a population of about 140,000. In late November the town centre already boasted a Christmas market, its colourful stalls redolent of ginger and cinnamon, hot wine and sausages.

We lived in Ermlandstrasse, in a highly bourgeois residential area twenty minutes by bus from the centre.

I lived my new life to an unprecedented schedule. I would get up at 7.30. After collecting the daily newspaper (the *Nordwest-Zeitung*) from the hall floor, I would make coffee. Anette and I would take breakfast together, upon which she would cycle to school and I would return to bed with my coffee and a book. Later, I would work on my latest composition; I also started writing a mock-gothic novel that eventually became *Death of a Medium*.

At lunchtime I might head into town to meet Anette and her friends, all prospective teachers and mostly encouragingly bibulous, for a drink and a bite to eat in Strohhalm ('drinking straw'), a friendly 'alternative' pub. Later I might browse around the bookshops, go to a library or take a walk in the beautiful Stadtpark. Then I would take the bus home, perhaps doze a little, work a little, and read a little. Then I would cook dinner. Anette taught me to prepare a variety of dishes: spaghetti bolognese, chilli con carne, stews with different kinds of sausage, and salads with proper homemade dressing – bottles of my beloved 'salad cream' being decisively and derisively *verboten*. She would return at around 7.00 p.m.; we would dine, then lie on the bed watching TV for the rest of the evening.

It was impossible to continue indefinitely without some kind of job, so I applied for a post teaching piano at the Oldenburger Musikschule. Not alone was my application successful, but on learning that I was a composer, the principal, Herr M., expanded my prospective title to 'professor of piano and composition'.

Herr M. was a boyish forty-something-year-old of trendy disposition. He peppered his conversation with slang words characteristic of *Jugendsprache* ('youthspeak'), such as *geil, super, ätzend*. Although I loathed this habit, I rather liked him; he radiated an infectious enthusiasm about music and music-teaching, and was well disposed towards contemporary music. Perhaps he was bored with the status quo and imagined that a neurotic foreign composer was just the person to liven things up.

It was, therefore, with a sense that my existence in Germany was acquiring a firm footing that I returned to Ireland with Anette that summer. We stayed with the Scottish conductor and composer William York who had recently founded the Dublin Sinfonia, a chamber orchestra specialising in contemporary music. We revisited old haunts and old friends, drank a lot, and finally paid a trip to Bunclody.

My father, a good judge of character, took to Anette at once and put her at her ease – a state of mind that my mother rapidly sought to dispel. She took Anette aside and told her that she was broken-hearted because I had lost my faith.

'Oh, um, I'm sorry to hear that, Mrs Deane...'

'Do you think there's any chance he might start going to mass again?'

'Um, I really don't know, Mrs Deane...'

'Would you encourage him to go, do you think?'

'I'm a Lutheran, Mrs Deane...'

'You're a what...?! Oh...I see.'

Naturally, I was obliged to sleep on the living room couch for the duration of our short stay, while Anette slept in what had been my room. Any other arrangement would have been inconceivable in the Ireland of those years, although were my parents alive today they would hardly countenance any less puritanical arrangement. Nonetheless, I returned to Oldenburg with a sense that this had been a successful holiday on every level.

I taught ten piano pupils weekly, on Thursday and Friday afternoons. They ranged in age from ten to twenty-six. The younger ones, I felt certain, were learning the piano as a social grace to please their status-conscious parents. Few showed signs of either talent or enthusiasm. The main interest in their lives was tennis, a game experiencing a surge of interest in Germany at that time thanks to the exploits of Boris Becker.

My favourite pupil was Bettina, a ten-year-old who had no gift for the piano but a powerful gift of the gab. Much of our time together was devoted to her detailed and possibly embroidered accounts of her adventures at school, spiced with colourful epithets directed at teachers or other children. After each of her sallies she would stop short with a sharp intake of breath, putting her tiny hand to her large mouth and opening her eyes very wide, as if in shock, before plunging onward with the same or another anecdote. The juicy word *Kotzbrocken* (literally 'lump of puke') rapidly entered my repertoire of invective, although much of what she so breathlessly related by-passed my still faltering German comprehension.

As my piano teaching was perhaps not the most efficient, the person who learned most from these classes was myself – and not just from a linguistic point of view. I had dreaded nothing so much as the regular encounter with small children, yet found that I related easily to them and they to me. I was informal in my approach, and disinclined to stand on my dignity. In turn, once they had sniffed me up and down, the kids seemed to locate a vestige of childishness in me that put them at ease.

Engaging socially with Germans on their own turf was often difficult. I grew accustomed to the fact that once introduced to strangers I would be ignored and studiously excluded from the conversation. No polite questions would be forthcoming about Ireland, about my own activities and views, or about my reactions to Germany. I tended to see this as a discourteous and self-centred indifference, but Anette interpreted it as fear that I might regard such probing as inquisitive. Certainly there was a clash of cultures involved, every bit as drastic as that pertaining between occidentals and orientals. I came to appreciate those qualities in the Irish, including their unabashed nosiness, that drew to our shores those Germans – including Anette herself – who had little patience with the more zipped-up traits of their compatriots.

One evening Anette and I were invited to dine at the home of one of her senior teaching colleagues. Arriving before our host had returned from work, we were greeted by his charming wife who served us aperitifs and chatted amiably and exclusively to Anette. At last the paterfamilias arrived and, after introductions, donned his slippers, seated himself in the only armchair, and diligently knitted some indeterminate garment while chatting exclusively to Anette.

After dinner our host had his guitar brought to him and called for '*die Gesangbücher*'. Three homemade songbooks, photocopied sheets of music stapled together, were produced by his obedient spouse. While the Herr Professor strummed manfully, the three of us attacked a succession of middle-of-the-road favourites. The wife's tremulous soprano led us upwards, I politely held the middle ground, while Anette's tuneless bass kept us rooted.

Of course, the Herr Professor was an honourable man and probably had decent progressive inclinations. Nonetheless, he gave me an extremely jaundiced perspective on middle-class, middle-aged German males.

My career continued to thrive, without my making any particular efforts to push it.

In the late spring of 1985 I learned that I had been awarded the Martin Toonder Award, funded by the Dutch humourist of that name who had lived in Ireland since 1965. This was regarded as the highest honour that could be bestowed upon an Irish artist. It was certainly the most lucrative, amounting to the then not insignificant sum of £3,000.

Meanwhile, I had been nominated by Gerard Victory and John Kinsella for membership of Aosdána, the government-sponsored academy of creative artists. As was more or less customary, this initial application failed; my zealous sponsors assured me that they would try again the following year.

I won the commission to write a piece for the London Sinfonietta, a chamber orchestra that was to make its Irish debut in the 1986 Dublin Festival of Twentieth Century Music. This was not all: in a further concert of chamber music to be played by members selected from the Sinfonietta, my first string quartet (*Silhouettes*) was to receive its premiere. Apparently

I was flavour of the month with that celebrated orchestra; it was, however, to be a short month.

The year 1985 was also the European Year of Music. RTÉ decided to celebrate it with a symphony concert consisting of three contemporary Irish works including my extravagant *Enchaînement*. This piece required the construction of an extension to the stage of the NCH and the importation of droves of string, wind and percussion players (no fewer than ten of the latter were required) from the UK. Thus my childhood fantasy of musical Cinerama was to be realised!

Anette and I returned to Dublin in late July in time for the *Enchaînement* performance, but not for rehearsals. Therefore I was unable to prevent the conductor, Colman Pearce, from separating three of the four sections of the piece, a misunderstanding due entirely to my failure to specify in the score that it was to be played without a break. I was distressed and angry, unreasonably unwilling to accept any responsibility for this blunder, and unforgivably curt with Pearce in the NCH bar afterwards. That night I was determined to drink myself into a stupor, whereas Anette and everyone else in the company (including my sister and some friends of hers who had travelled all the way from Switzerland) wanted an early night. There was bad feeling all round, and I was making myself very unpopular.

Next day my brother John was to drive us to Bunclody, but I was too sick to travel. Anette, who was understandably fed up with me, opted to go without me although this meant several days dealing with my mother's anxious questions concerning my physical and spiritual welfare. When I eventually returned to the fold I was made to feel far from welcome, and what should have been a triumphal visit turned instead into a debacle.

Anette made me promise that henceforth I would touch no alcohol before 6.00 p.m. and entirely foreswear spirits. Reluctantly I complied but, as anyone with any experience of alcoholism knows, such promises and stratagems are worthless. If drink could be said to have consistently vied with Anette for my affections, my relationship with Dame Ethyl now frequently took on the character of an illicit affair as I took every opportunity to circumvent both promises. With the contorted logic of the drunkard, I felt deepening resentment that I was obliged to resort to such deceit in the first place, while Anette gradually lost whatever trust she had still invested in me.

Back in Germany I embarked without enthusiasm on my second year of teaching. I completed my *De/montage* for the London Sinfonietta, and embarked on a *Chamber Concertino* commissioned by William York for the Dublin Sinfonia.

Anette finished her teacher training and was now vainly looking for a full-time job. For very little money she taught several hours a week in a 'gruesome' (her word) language school run by a dapper Mexican called, of course, Manuel. She was discontented and frustrated, and the atmosphere between us became increasingly fraught.

In November 1985 I gave an illustrated talk on my work in Oldenburg University. This had been arranged by the professor of composition there, Gustavo Becerra-Schmidt (1925-2010). He was an exiled Chilean composer to whom I had at some point introduced myself, a good-natured humanist of pronounced leftist views. He introduced me to the small audience as 'someone who, more than any composer I know, sees music as a call (*Ruf*) rather than a profession (*Beruf*)'. He went on to express the hope that I would explain why I, a Stockhausen pupil, 'had abandoned the *avant-garde*'.

I was surprised by these propositions, neither of which was entirely welcome to me. Without having reflected much on the question, I regarded myself as a 'professional' composer.

As for 'abandoning the *avant-garde*', with even less reflection I still regarded myself as belonging to that nebulous club. Becerra-Schmidt's well-meaning phrase caused me to wonder whether I should not radicalise myself a bit. This suggests that I was still quite uncertain about the direction my work should be taking.

 کی   کی   کی

The 1986 Dublin Festival of Twentieth Century Music was cancelled, never to be revived. The London Sinfonietta did not travel to Dublin, and neither *De/montage* nor *Silhouettes* received its premiere.

I wrote to Elgar Howarth, who was to have conducted *De/montage*, asking whether the orchestra would nonetheless schedule a performance of the work, given that it had commissioned it. He replied (in those days people still replied to letters) that he knew nothing about the matter and that it had nothing to do with him.

Here, then, was a disaster that, for once, was not of my making. It proved that fate was against me and gave me an excuse to drown my sorrows with the potent *Weizenbier* (wheat beer) to which I had lately become addicted.

Because of teaching duties, I had decided not to travel to Dublin for the premiere of my *Chamber Concertino*. However, the night before this performance I had a drunken quarrel with Anette about nothing of any significance. In my fury I had leapt out of bed, tripped, and struck my head against the sharp edge of a loudspeaker. After a night spent sulking on the floor, I had stormed into the city and booked a one-way flight to Dublin at great expense, having first had my latest head-wound cleaned and bandaged in a pharmacy.

I flew from Bremen, arriving in Dublin in a fragile state but in time for the two performances of the *Concertino*, one in each half of a very demanding concert that took place in the historic Peppercanister Church. Afterwards I continued drinking with William York and the English composer David Bedford, whose *Symphony* had also been played. The session was continued in William's flat, where I woke up next day with a violent hangover and very unclear memories of the previous evening.

In the course of the morning Anette rang, correctly guessing where I had ended up. She coldly assured me that she would ring the Musikschule and make my excuses, and would expect me back within the next few days.

By the time I returned to Oldenburg I had spent an inordinate amount of money on two last-minute flights, blackened my reputation still further with the Musikschule where the principal had already warned me about my level of absenteeism, made a fool of myself in Dublin, deepened the chasm between myself and Anette, and further undermined the crumbling edifice of my so recently reconstituted self-respect. The successful premiere of a large-scale new work seemed an irrelevance in comparison to these calamities.

Two further events of some importance occurred that spring.

Firstly, I was elected to Aosdána thanks to the renewed efforts of Messrs Victory and Kinsella. Although I feigned to regard this as a triviality, I was secretly gratified by such peer recognition at a time when insecurity was again threatening to drown me. Secondly, Anette moved to Cologne. She had given up on the likelihood of employment as a teacher and had opted for additional training as a journalist. Although we agreed that I should join her as soon as my teaching year was over, the air was filled with portents of separation.

Chapter 22

I now saw myself as 'serving out my sentence' in the Musik-schule, while exempt from the restrictions on my drinking previously agreed between myself and Anette. I started each day with a few glasses of wine, the better to counteract the ill effects of the previous day's carousing. If I turned up to teach at all, it was usually in a befuddled state. Pupils, not surprisingly, began staying away from classes. I spent hours sitting at the piano in my hated room at the school, playing very badly pieces that I could normally play quite well, and chewing packet after packet of mints in the vain hope that no other member of staff would smell liquor on my breath.

I was spared the almost inevitable indignity of dismissal when I emerged from my stupor one morning suffering from a burning itch in the region of my belly. On pulling down the sheets I saw an angry rash of blistered red patches across my gut. The rational option would have been to visit the doctor without delay. The irrational option was the one I took: I drank several glasses of wine in the hope of falling asleep. Maybe on waking I would find that this new plague had vanished, or been nothing but a hallucination.

The burning discomfort kept me awake, however, so in the afternoon I got dressed, packed a bag, and set out for Cologne.

Unsteadily, I found my way to the Nippes district, where Anette had found a flat.

Less than overjoyed to see me, Anette identified my condition as shingles, an adult offshoot of the chickenpox virus. We visited the out-patient department of a local hospital where this diagnosis was confirmed and the appropriate medication and dressings provided.

Back in Oldenburg I obtained leave from school and stocked up on alcohol. There ensued a period that is a complete black hole in my memory. At some point I emerged from that hole to make a despairing telephone call to my sister in Paris. Convinced that I was dying, she booked the first available flight to Bremen. This was so imminent that she was obliged to hire a helicopter to bring her from her workplace, the UNESCO building, to Orly Airport.

On arrival in Oldenburg she found not a mouldering corpse but a mouldy composer (in the Irish sense of the adjective: hopelessly intoxicated) eager for a night on the town. Too relieved to be incensed, Patricia agreed to this plan; next day, however, she escorted me to hospital where she explained in her fluent German that I was drinking uncontrollably, subject to extreme panic attacks, and possibly suicidal.

Were this Ireland I would now have been sedated and allowed to sleep for a day or two. Being dour northwestern Germany, I was kept under close observation but obliged to go 'cold turkey'. I was fed, given injections of vitamins, and forced to use an exercise bicycle (dark thoughts of Nazi torture chambers flitting through my addled brain). Sleeping tablets were strictly forbidden.

On the third night, as I tossed and turned and sweated and shook, a sympathetic night nurse, warning me not to betray her, fed me two sleeping pills. At last I got a few hours' fitful rest.

A colleague from the Musikschule visited me, conveying Herr M.'s best wishes, and agreeing to convey my message that I would be unable to return to work. He kindly gave me a second-hand copy of Joseph Conrad's *Lord Jim*, in English. Learning from the introduction that Conrad had had vacillating views on the order of the novel's two parts, I read it in both versions on successive days.

After just over a week I was released. In terms recalling those used by his Morlaix colleague, a severe young doctor (dark thoughts of Mengele flitting through my brain) warned me that henceforth I should drink nothing stronger than water. On learning that I planned to move to Cologne and that I contemptuously dismissed Alcoholics Anonymous as a bunch of religious maniacs, he gave me the address of an organisation called The Good Templars, an international temperance organisation supposedly free of religious overtones. Insincerely, I promised him I would look them up.

I left the hospital feeling fit as a fiddle, and made straight for the nearest Greek restaurant. I ordered neither beer nor *retsina*, and felt uncommonly virtuous as I spurned the complimentary glass of Ouzo, with which my waiter attempted to lure me from the new-found path of virtue, with the treacherously over-confident words '*ich trinke kein Alkohol!*' ('I drink no alcohol!').

At the beginning of May, shortly after the third anniversary of my first encounter with Anette, I travelled to Cologne with two suitcases and only the slightest hope that I could salvage our relationship. I signed on with social welfare, and set about trying to lead as quiet a life as possible.

Anette's flat was in Cranachstrasse, on the second floor of a building that housed a second-hand bookshop which would provide most of my reading material for the next few months.

One wall of the living room was wallpapered with the vastly blown-up colour photograph of an idyllic mountain landscape dominated by a waterfall. The bathroom, ominously reminiscent of Berlin, was on the first floor landing. These two factors suggested that Anette had not been spoilt for choice when she went apartment hunting, and that she saw the place as merely a temporary refuge.

My resolution to stay sober did not last long, but the frantic dissipation of my last months in Oldenburg abated. I made no attempt to re-establish links with any of the Cologne-based composers I had known a decade earlier, with the exception of my old friend Clarence who now also lived in Nippes. He had in fact harboured Anette while she sought an apartment.

Anette and I lived on together in what amounted to a fragile truce, neither of us quite willing to sever the link definitively. On my part this reluctance stemmed from a mixture of dependence and the fear of starting from scratch after the failure of my most sustained attempt to reform my existence, something I still could not concede was incompatible with continued alcohol abuse. On her part, the unwillingness stemmed from habit, and perhaps a touch of pity. And undoubtedly there were the lingering traces of a strong affection.

At last a telephone call forced me back to Ireland. My mother was seriously ill in a hospital in Enniscorthy, County Wexford, and was not expected to survive. By the time I arrived there she had no idea who I or anybody else was, with the exception of my father. Indeed, that was but a partial exception, for the 'Don' whom she greeted so affectionately, whose hand she held so girlishly as he sat on the side of her bed, and who in turn addressed her so lovingly as 'Josie', a version of her name I had never heard before, was not the bald 78-year-old whom the rest of us saw, but the tall, mischievous gallant who had courted her to the disapproval of her family almost forty years before.

Lung cancer, and the morphine used to palliate its devastation, had stripped away her memories but had also pushed aside those harsher layers of personality that had accrued in the decades since her young womanhood. Josie was playful to the point of flirtatiousness. Introduced anew to her own children each time they visited, she was courteous and completely unfazed by the revelation, daily renewed, that she had borne and raised us.

It is idle but irresistible to imagine how things might have been in our household had this warm and playful individual, first revealed to her children on her deathbed, not acquired the defensive and forbidding carapace that would later make intimacy with her so difficult. But perhaps we were all to blame for not having been able to intuit and nurture it earlier.

Half way through that afflicting week, Declan arrived back from the USA where he had been living for some years.

'And who is this fine young man?' she inquired breezily.

'I'm your eldest son, Declan.'

'Oh, really? Well, you're very welcome! And what do you do?'

'I baptize people, and marry them, and give them Holy Communion.'

A pause during which she registered and processed this information. Then she pursed her lips and her tone of voice hardened.

'You mean you're a priest?'

'That's right.'

'Then why aren't you wearing your Roman collar!?'

For a moment the Catholic reactionary was back in control, forever outraged by something or other, before retreating forever into the recesses of dementia.

As each visit neared its close, a scintilla of panic would enter her fading eyes. At first she would remonstrate with us. On being told that the nurse was throwing us out, she would plead to be taken home. We explained that this was impossible, that we would not be able to take care of her, and that she would be in great pain.

'But I feel fine. There's no pain whatever.'

'That's because of the pills you're taking.'

'What pills? Nobody has given me any pills!'

The nightly repetition of this ritual was an ordeal for all of us, but must have caused our father the most unspeakable torment. Although I was snared in my own emotional trap, I tried to imagine his grief and to reach out to him, but he was inaccessible, and would sit all day by the fire gazing into the flames, into the past, longing for and dreading the evening.

I had been commissioned by Lontano, a London group, to compose a string trio for their forthcoming Irish tour and I worked on it steadily during that week. Of all my works it most clearly reflects that urge to be 'more *avant-garde*' inadvertently instilled in me by Becerra-Schmidt in Oldenburg. *Écarts* is a piece about separation, based largely on the *Farewell* section of Beethoven's *Les adieux* piano sonata. On the evening of my mother's death I composed her initials J.D into the score, which I completed soon afterwards.

That night my father sat silently, occasionally placing a briquette on the fire. At a moment when only I was present he suddenly burst into tears and began to lament.

'Oh Josie, Josie, why have you gone and left me here on my own?'

For a moment something unfathomable was in the room, something so archaic that my father no longer seemed a being of flesh and blood but an embodiment of lamentation. Putting my arm clumsily around his shoulder I said, 'you're not on your own'. But he was, and so was I.

At the funeral mass in Bunclody Church I was the organist. I played the Prelude to Wagner's *Lohengrin* and the slow movement theme from Scriabin's *Piano Concerto*. These may seem like irreverent, even mischievous choices. To me, however, they were among the most beautiful moments in music and were therefore appropriate. Five years later, in the same place, I played the same music to commemorate my father.

Throughout that melancholy Christmas, although I had drunk the occasional beer in company with my siblings and other mourners, I had remained sober and had behaved responsibly to a degree that surprised everybody, but most of all myself. Now I determined to restart my life, and perhaps one day become worthy of Anette's trust again.

At the beginning of 1987 I received the first quarterly payment of my allowance (or *cnuas*, a Gaelic word for 'treasure') as an Aosdána member. Of course the possession of a modest regular income that did not require my presence at a place of employment was a great danger, and one with which I at first coped badly. My life see-sawed between drinking bouts in Dublin and lengthy periods of recuperation in Bunclody.

During one of these periods, sudden and severe back pains obliged me to visit a local doctor. Having diagnosed a kidney infection and issued the appropriate prescription, this frustrated rural Freud detected some deeper malaise which he rapidly deduced was related to alcohol. He prescribed psychotropic (mind-altering) pills that had just come on the market. I was to take one a day with water, but *under no circumstances* was I to consume alcohol during the period of treatment.

As long as I remained in Bunclody this injunction was easily obeyed. But as my mood lightened, partly thanks to the magic yellow capsules, I resolved to return to Cologne to 'collect my things' and try my luck with Anette once more. Naturally this entailed a stay of several days in Dublin where I again started drinking, confident that the innocent country doctor had exaggerated the possible risks.

He had not. By the time I arrived in Germany strange things had started happening in my head, sporadic visual and auditory hallucinations reminiscent of delirium tremens but without the accompanying aura of menace and panic.

If I now expected Anette to fall into my arms and declare her renewed faith in me because I was seeking to medicate away my problems, I was sorely mistaken. I was hurt that she did not appreciate the efforts I was making, and resented the thought that she made no allowances for the grief occasioned by my mother's death (I easily convinced myself of the sincerity of this cynical piece of emotional exploitation). One night, after a particularly bitter row in the course of which I was continually distracted by imaginary voices from the neighbouring kitchen, I barricaded myself into the guest bedroom with a bottle of wine, consumed the remainder of my lethal yellow capsules (I believe there were thirteen left), and once again prepared to die.

Instead, I slept until the following afternoon and awoke convinced that I had important tasks to perform. I showered and shaved, and made my way to a suburban area of Cologne entirely unfamiliar to me. On arrival, I could not recall the vital errand that had brought me there. I wandered serenely around the leafy streets, convinced that some landmark would remind me.

At last an Italian restaurant reminded me that I had eaten nothing in two days. I installed myself and ordered food and wine. As I ate and drank I noticed the strange fact that all diners in the crowded restaurant were speaking English, and that by singling out individual tables I could hear every word of the conversations taking place. Strangely enough, Ireland was in each case the subject under discussion. However, it was at the neighbouring table that the most significant and, frankly, unacceptable things were being said: all four diners were insulting my native country in the most sarcastic terms and, what's more, they were saying objectionable things about myself!

I paid the bill, stood up and addressed them unceremoniously. In English I informed them that they knew nothing about Ireland, they knew nothing about me, and clearly knew nothing about anything – typical Germans! With this *coup de grâce* I strode out of the restaurant, highly pleased with myself and proud of my patriotism.

I renewed my aimless ramblings through the now dark streets, all thoughts of an urgent errand forgotten. When I came to an *U-Bahn* station I made my way back to Nippes, drank the stale wine remaining from the previous night's suicide attempt, and slept for another seventeen or eighteen hours. The next evening my head had cleared considerably, and although I could still occasionally hear voices, I now accepted – with curious equanimity – that they were imaginary.

A few days later, still confused but convinced that the link with Anette had been definitively broken, I packed my bags, bade her a tearful farewell, and returned to Dublin. I was determined never to set foot in Germany again.

The country doctor pursed his lips when I gave him an expurgated account of these hallucinatory events. Nothing daunted, and with renewed words of warning, he wrote another prescription for those same magic yellow capsules.

I went to Dublin to attend a rehearsal and the premiere of *Écarts*, which took place on 1 March in the Royal Hospital Kilmainham, a beautiful seventeenth century building restored in 1984 to house the Irish Museum of Modern Art.

During this period I stayed with a friend in Rathmines. Greatly concerned for my welfare, she ensured that I turned up at the rehearsal, and attended the concert with me. She was unable to prevent my being almost comatose at this event, but later that evening she asked to see the pills that I was taking. When I produced the bottle she snatched it and flushed its remaining contents down the lavatory. Perhaps she saved my life with this presumptuous and unilateral gesture! Of course I failed to thank her for it, as I had failed to thank so many other people for so many other kindnesses.

A few days later, having regathered my forces in Bunclody, I returned to Dublin for a photo opportunity. I had just received my most significant commission to date: for an orchestral composition to celebrate the capital city's purported millennium in 1988. I was to be presented with an envelope ostensibly containing the £3,000 I had been awarded – a considerable sum for a commission in those days – by the Lord Mayor of Dublin Bertie Ahern who would become Taoiseach (Prime Minister) a decade later.

The ceremony was to take place outside the Custom House at 9.00 a.m., so I booked myself into a nearby bed & breakfast the previous night. I visited a local pub and sat down in a corner with my book and a pint, feeling on top of the world and delighted to be liberated from the psychotropic yellow capsules. As the night drew on, I was engaged in conversation by a man of my own age who, as it happened, was staying in the same B&B as myself. At closing time, reluctant to let the night have the last word, we agreed to go halves on a bottle of whiskey which we brought back to his room.

I cannot recall what weighty subjects we discussed, and I cannot guarantee that at some point we did not burst into a round of rebel songs. The next thing I remember is being woken by my alarm clock at 7.30 a.m. On the chair beside my bed sat an empty whiskey bottle and a half-full glass of whiskey, which I drank at a gulp. I was fully clothed and had wet myself.

I rushed to the bathroom in groggy consternation and cleaned myself up as best I could. Without shaving, forsaking breakfast, I hastened to the nearest early morning pub – The Master Mariner in Store Street, where I suspect my father had not been unknown – and tossed down three double vodkas.

In this dishevelled, bleary and malodorous condition I was photographed accepting an empty envelope from the future Prime Minister, who pretended alternately to play a trumpet and a clarinet. These excruciating images subsequently appeared in several daily newspapers and in the *RTÉ Guide*. My father diligently cut them from the latter and from the *Irish Independent*, dated them in his spidery handwriting, and handed them to me without comment when I went home a few days later.

Chapter 23

That April I moved into a first-floor bedsit overlooking Upper Leeson Street.

Increasingly, I concentrated my drinking on Grogans, a famously bohemian public house presided over by the legendary Paddy O'Brien, a man who had served and refused service to Patrick Kavanagh, and who was benignly disposed towards me.

Here I fell among thieves, and not just in the figurative sense. Among the hardened drinkers who became my regular cronies was Danny, a dapper rogue with an enviable way with women and an unenviable prison record. Danny rapidly ascertained that I possessed a cheque book, and seemed convinced that it was intended primarily for his benefit. He would play chess with me on my tiny portable set and would cheat shamelessly and without subtlety, taking back moves and moving pieces around when my back was turned. Eventually, when I tired of this and told him I would play no more, he simply appropriated the set and found other victims.

A more congenial companion was my old friend John Jordan. Nowadays, frustratingly, he lapsed into a comatose state after one or two drinks. John had a fine mind, had known everyone worth knowing, and could, when he wished, converse with an eloquence that contrasted blatantly with the drivel spouted by most of my associates. He was a generous man who, when *compos mentis*, would always stand me a pint or a short. On seeing me he would invariably exclaim 'Ravel! *Ma mere l'oye!*' and reminisce fondly about Annaghmakerrig.

No matter how shaky I felt, I was never too self-conscious to sidle into Grogans and sit in a dark corner with a pint of water until such time as a willing victim entered the premises and either plied me with drink or 'lent' me money (or both).

Sometimes Paddy O'Brien or Tommy Smith, one of the pub's co-proprietors, would let me have a few drinks on the house. When my cheques bounced they did not make too much of an issue of it, although they kept a tab of what I owed them.

Of course, I had a major orchestral work to write, and this necessitated periodic trips to Bunclody. Whether I arrived drunk, hungover or semi-sober, my father always met me at the bus stop and was always welcoming and non-judgmental. He would 'feed me up' and slip me a few pounds when I left.

That summer my drinking, already excessive, took a turn for the worse. It required increasing quantities of alcohol to relieve the horror of my hangovers, yet my capacity for the stuff was diminishing drastically. This meant that by the time I had begun to feel semi-human, usually in the early afternoon, I was ready to stagger home and collapse into a short-lived and unrefreshing stupor. At 7.00 or 8.00 p.m. I would emerge from this with a fully reconstituted hangover, and start the whole awful process again.

This harrowing schedule often entailed waking during 'the hour of the wolf', at 3.00 or 4.00 a.m. Unable to get back to sleep I would lie there until morning, racked with anxiety, soaked in perspiration, trembling, nauseated, and dreading the *delirium tremens* that somehow remained at bay.

I ate little, although sometimes Danny dragged me into a restaurant during the 'holy hour' when he would eat with a

while I picked at a snack and concentrated
the wine. I would pay for this with a cheque,
had the funds to cover it.

I lurched homewards I collapsed somewhere
et.

find myself in bed in an unknown environment.
Someone had apparently taken the unacceptable liberty of in-
serting a wire into my penis. When I sought to remove it, my
hand was clasped by an attractive young woman in a white uniform, whose firm but gentle words were: 'Don't – it'll be very
sore.'

I drifted back into pleasing unconsciousness. When I came
to, I was in a different bed, surrounded by curtains. My body
was free of intrusive appendages. I felt drained but peaceful,
and sought in vain to remember how I had arrived wherever
I was.

The curtains were drawn aside and a doctor materialised.
He told me I was in Saint Vincent's Hospital, an ambulance
having picked me off the street three days earlier. I had suffered an epileptic fit, and been 'transferred to Casualty comatose, feverish, with abnormally low blood pressure and a
severe metabolic acidosis', to quote the medical records that
I accessed a quarter century later (metabolic acidosis is an excess of acid in the body fluids). I was also suffering from dangerously rapid heart rhythm. On resuscitation I had been able
to inform them that I had been drinking an average of ten pints
of beer daily prior to my collapse (a figure plucked out of the
air, and omitting any reference to wine, vodka and whiskey).

Growing increasingly agitated over the following days I had
been heavily sedated and indeed 'became unrousable due to
excess sedation', which necessitated my transfer to intensive
care.

The words that most horrified me were 'epileptic fit'. The doctor reassured me that I was not an epileptic, and the fit I had suffered was probably due to withdrawal from alcohol; such fits need not recur were I to avoid getting into such a state again.

Later that day my father visited me, bringing me a copy of Thomas Flanagan's novel *The Year of the French*, which turned out to be an excellent piece of hospital reading. He had been summoned by the hospital when it seemed that my life was in danger (interestingly, this is not mentioned in the medical records). Of course, he had been terribly worried but, he gently concluded, I was better now, and perhaps this was the shock that would lead to my changing my life... Yes, I responded fervently, definitely! I had learned my lesson, and everything would be different from now on.

I was taken for an endoscopy. Liquid Valium was injected into my arm to sedate me while a tube was inserted down my throat to ascertain the condition of my gastro-intestinal tract. I coughed and retched and sweated and sobbed. The doctor, disconcerted, ordered more Valium, to no avail; I went on retching and weeping until the procedure was finished. An hour later the doctor visited me, expecting to find me in a state of unconsciousness. Instead, I was sitting up in bed reading *The Year of the French*. He appeared baffled, and almost disapproving. The medical records mention Valium, but not my failure to respond to it.

My stomach was fine, and a biopsy revealed that my liver was 'as well as could be expected', and would undoubtedly recover fully 'if I gave it a chance'. Had this latest and most spectacular collapse not occurred on the street but while I was at home, nobody would have known about it and I would certainly have died.

Of course, I emerged from hospital a new man. I had seen the error of my ways and henceforth would shun the embrace of Dame Ethyl. I had no fewer than three lucrative commissions waiting for me and I completed them, working mainly in Bunclody, in an unprecedented spate of concentrated work. These, like *Écarts*, were *avant-garde* pieces, quite remote in style from my earlier (and later) works, but effective for all that.

I was busy, healthy, sober and making money. Each evening I went on a pub crawl, drinking litres of non-alcoholic beer just to prove that I could resist temptation. Once more I anticipated amorous adventures and was undaunted when they failed to materialise – after all, it was just a matter of time until Anette and I were reunited.

We agreed to spend a week together in the Canary Islands that autumn. On 4 November I flew to Gran Canaria, where she had booked us into a German holiday resort (where the restaurants advertised *Kaffee wie zu Hause!* – 'coffee just like at home!'). We were reasonably at ease with one another, although I felt from the start that she was insufficiently appreciative of my self-reforming zeal. I half hoped that she might confine her drinking to mineral water in solidarity with my virtuous abstemiousness. I resented the pleasure she clearly derived from a glass of wine with her meals, and envied her ability to slake her thirst in this warm climate with glasses of cool, refreshing, tempting beer.

We visited the Playa del Inglés and sneered at the crass loutishness of the Brits. We swam twice a day. We hired a car one rainy day and drove into the mountains, terrified by the absence of barriers on the abyss side of the wet winding road (lucky Anette could calm herself afterwards with a cool, refreshing, tempting beer). We took a boat trip to Tenerife, where I admired the snow-capped volcano and fantasised that it was the Popocatepetl of *Under the Volcano*.

As the holiday wound to a close, it became clear that it would not give renewed impetus to our relationship. I believed that I had proved my readiness to change my life in the interests of such a renewal, but that she was unwilling to meet me half way. I felt cheated, and bitterly resentful. We were leaving on successive days, so I saw her off at the airport, continued by bus to Palma, and booked into a hotel. Soon I was sitting at a terrace overlooking the sea, a large, cool, refreshing beer in front of me.

Four months without alcohol had toughened my system, so that it took a while for me to disintegrate again. After Gran Canaria I practically severed contact with the rest of my family. I learned that my father was spending Christmas in Dublin with John and his new wife Ursula, but there was no question of my inviting myself around. Instead, I accepted an invitation from the poet Michael Hartnett to partake of Christmas dinner in his house, which was a few doors away from my Leeson Street bedsit. When I arrived, Michael nervously ushered me into his sitting room, where the table was laid for one. He himself was on the dry and his wife, fearing contagion, had ordained that I should eat alone, be given one single glass of whiskey, and sent on my way. The impulse to walk out in a dignified huff seized me momentarily, but I had little dignity left, was hungry, and 'had a mind for a dhrop'.

A week later my Dublin Millennium piece, *Thresholds*, was performed at the NCH, conducted by Proinnsías Ó Duinn. I had attended no rehearsals. I sat in the reserved seats with a retinue of Groganites, as the habitués of that drinking establishment are known. After the concert I refused to see in the New Year with any of the musicians or even to congratulate Prionnsías on his exertions.

The year began in a blur and degenerated steadily. I stopped shaving, and took to sleeping fully clothed on the couches or floors of various cronies' flats, which were mostly dirty and often stank. I began to smoke heavily and soon had acquired my first and last nicotine stains.

On my birthday, 27 January, I trundled homewards before the holy hour and decided to have a quick drink in O'Dwyer's at Leeson Street Bridge.

'A pint of Smithwicks, please.'

'I'm sorry, we're all out of Smithwicks.'

'Oh? A pint of Harp then.'

'Sorry, there's not a drop left.'

'Guinness?'

'All gone.'

I gazed at the flippant young man, and noticed my image in the mirror behind him.

'Look, I know I look a bit ratty because I haven't shaved in a while, but today's my birthday...'

'Happy birthday, then. Maybe you'd be better off going home for a nap.'

I went around the corner into the neighbouring pub, O'Brien's.

'A pint of Smithwicks, please.'

'I'm afraid we're all out of it, sir.'

I bought a half bottle of vodka in the nearest off-licence and went home. I had broken my last remaining glass, so I mixed the vodka with water and sipped it gloomily out of a cup. If desperation mixed with desolation has a taste, then this was it.

In March I spent two weeks in Annaghmakerrig. I fell in love with two women, but was too shaky to make advances to them. For the first time the Centre and its idyllic surroundings failed to work their magic on me, and although the manuscript paper sat expectantly on my work table I failed to compose any music. The sense that I was written out, at a time when my stipend as an Aosdána member imposed an obligation on me to be productive, intensified my sense of gloom and anxiety.

April Fool's Day arrived and with it my second instalment of the *Cnuas*. For a few days I brightened up, and ate a couple of solid meals. I contemplated shaving, but decided that my hand shook too much. I bought a ruinous piano for £300 and had it transported to Upper Leeson Street. However, the staircase was too narrow to accommodate it so the movers left it sitting in the front hall. This enraged my landlady, whose permission to import it I had not sought in the first place, and I was instructed to have it removed as soon as possible.

Shortly thereafter I arrived back with a bottle of whiskey and a woman. She had not accompanied me for romantic reasons but because, herself an alcoholic and depressive, she had been thrown out of her own lodgings.

We drank, we smoked, I vainly attempted to seduce her, we drank and smoked some more, and I passed out.

It was daylight when I woke up on my own, lying on the floor. My clothes were wet and the fringes of my sweater were charred, a fact possibly not unconnected to the smell of smoke in the air. I would have transferred myself to the bed but, oddly enough, it was no longer there. The wallpaper behind it had turned black. I changed into dry clothes and crept out of the room. The landing window was wide open, and when I looked through it I beheld a charred mattress smoking on the back lawn.

Attempting to tiptoe past the piano in the hallway I was accosted by my landlady. She was not exactly *irate*, the adjective usually deemed appropriate in these circumstances, but seemed to have passed through that state to arrive at a condition of quiet stoicism.

'What happened last night?' I inquired, in the tremulous tones of one who really does not want to know.

'Either you or your female companion, who should not have been there in the first place, fell asleep holding a lighted cigarette. The bed went on fire. Fortunately I smelt the smoke, got in, and put out the blaze with a fire extinguisher. Your companion – who seemed like a nice girl – (her harsh tones unambiguously conveyed an unflattering comparison with myself) had to be taken to hospital. You just lay down on the floor and went back to sleep.'

'Oh dear. What can I say? I'm very sorry.'

'I think we both of us know that you need to leave, as soon as possible, and take that piano with you.'

I left. Miraculously, I immediately found another place and without transition moved myself and the piano into it. This was a ground-floor flat in Lower Pembroke Street, near Fitzwilliam Square. I have never understood how the landlord, a gruff solicitor from Northern Ireland whose office was in the same building, agreed to let the place to someone as shabby and shaky as myself. Perhaps he was influenced by the fact that I produced a chequebook and bank card, and was able to pay a deposit and one month's rent in advance.

Installed in Pembroke Street, appreciably closer to Grogans, I took up where I had left off.

I discovered a magical ATM around the corner in Merrion Row. Each time that I withdrew money from it the amount on my advice slip would increase by the sum I had withdrawn, instead of decreasing! I watched *ordinary* people use this machine without displaying any signs of surprise or delight, and decided that for some reason the God of banking had singled me out.

But one evening the wonderful machine refused to give me anything. The sickly green letters on its screen formed words that told me I had 'exceeded my overdraft allowance'. Having long since lost my glasses, I had failed to notice the tiny minus sign to the left of the figures on my advice slips.

If my mind was no longer at home in the real world of pluses and minuses, my body was also growing increasingly alienated. I would practically crawl to Grogans, keeping as close to the buildings and as far from the kerb as possible for fear I would topple into the street and be crushed by a passing vehicle. I wished to die, yes, but not in such a grisly way. Lacking the energy to do away with myself, whenever and wherever I lay my body down to sleep I would pray to a God in whom I did not believe that He, She or It would let me sleep deeply and never wake up again. Yet either I failed to sleep, or woke up bitterly disappointed by the fact that I was still alive.

I had almost stopped eating, yet each day I would be racked by bouts of dry heaving, and it was rare for these ordeals to end without at least a few drops of blood bespattering the toilet bowl.

When June's rent came due, I wrote a cheque for the landlord in full knowledge that it would not be honoured. So terrified was I now of meeting that stern gentleman that I stayed away from the flat as much as possible, sometimes attempting to sleep off my morning's drinking in Stephen's Green rather than in my bed. If rain or illness forced me to stay at home, I would keep the blankets pulled over my head and not answer any knock at the door, no matter how peremptory.

Early in June John Jordan died at the Merriman Summer School in Wales. Although for years he had seemed like an old man, he was only fifty-eight. I grieved for him, and even attended his memorial service at Mount Argus Cemetery, an almost superhuman effort.

In my mind the droning of the priest was obliterated by John's cultured and gentle voice reciting Kavanagh's words: 'let grief be a fallen leaf at the dawning of the day.'

I was almost a tramp. I had no friends, only drinking companions. To all intents and purposes I had no family, for if my kin had not formally disowned me, I had put a barrier between us that shame and humiliation would no longer let me cross.

This, then, was rock bottom. I had not slit my wrists or taken an overdose of yellow pills. I had not recently suffered *delirium tremens* or epilepsy. But I was flayed and empty, barely alive.

ڪ   ڪ   ڪ

And then Bloomsday came. On 16 June Kennedy's of Westland Row was selling pints of Guinness for one 1904 penny, in honour of the day and the year on which Joyce's *Ulysses* is set. One could buy these coins for fifty new pence, and somehow I had acquired £5 worth of them, tantamount to ten pints and probable oblivion.

From Grogans to Kennedy's is not exactly a marathon hike. At 5.00 p.m. I set out with three or four other hard men. I could scarcely feel my extremities, and pins and needles ran up and down my legs. Descending Grafton Street, I was obliged to stop at regular intervals and hold on to a lamppost or litter bin. At last two of my comrades impatiently linked my arms and half carried me along by the side wall of Trinity, past the Lincoln Inn, and into the crowded but welcoming refuge of Kennedy's, where sixteen years earlier the AYIC had met and caroused and quarrelled.

Somehow we found seats, and I handed someone a precious 1904 penny. To my delight and relief it was soon exchanged for a black, foaming pint. I sipped it slowly, and gradually realised that I would be able to keep it down, by no means a foregone conclusion. I sipped some more, listened vacantly to the words of literary wisdom being exchanged by my companions, and watched with mild contempt the would-be Joyceans in their silly straw hats and striped jackets.

I finished my pint, handed another antique penny to a friend, and waited for the next pint. But calamity struck! Apparently the deal was that only one pint would be exchanged for one penny per person. The staff were keeping eagle eyes on the proceedings, and had observed that the Groganites had already had their quota.

What was to be done? We could possibly reconnoitre the other drinkers, people mostly unknown to us, and ask those who were not drinking Guinness if they would oblige us by taking our 1904 coins to the bar and...

No, no, no! Suddenly I was laughing inwardly as I had not laughed in a long time. By the lanky ghost of Jimmy Joyce, but it was farcical! Suddenly I felt light-headed and decisive all at once, an intoxication that was quite unlike that offered by Arthur Guinness or any of his colleagues. I had had enough!

I vacated my seat and went to the telephone. I dialled 999 and asked for an ambulance to be sent to Kennedy's Pub, Westland Row. I stood outside the main door and waited, and in a few minutes the ambulance arrived and an orderly leaped out.

'Is there an emergency here?'

'There is indeed – it's me.'

'You?'

I explained that I wished to stop drinking, and that I needed to go to hospital, and that I was barely capable of walking any more.

'Are you joking me?'

'I'm not.'

'Look, we only take emergency patients to Saint Vincent's tonight. That's not what you're looking for. You need Saint Pat's or John of God's!'

'Can you take me to either of those places?'

The young man looked hard at me, possibly wondering whether he should be angry, and deciding to be amused instead. Perhaps they had been having a quiet evening.

'Look, take a taxi. I wish you the best of luck, but we're only taking people to Vincent's.'

With that he leaped back into the ambulance, which drove off at high speed.

I returned to the pub and told one of my companions what had happened.

'Are you sure that you really want to do this?'

'I am.'

'OK, I'll bring you to St Pat's in a taxi if you pay for it.'

'I only have some 1904 pennies...' (Inwardly I was laughing...)

'But you have a chequebook.'

'I've one cheque left, and it's worthless.'

'No matter, Paddy O'Brien will cash it.'

While my companion fetched a taxi I painstakingly wrote myself a cheque for £10. We drove to Grogans where Paddy O'Brien exchanged the phoney cheque for a genuine £10.00 note.

We drove to Saint Patrick's Hospital, where I was admitted after some disputation, given that no doctor had referred me. My friend kept the change from my £10.00: he had earned it.

Thus it was that my last alcoholic drink cost me one 1904 penny.

Epilogue

He gave the little Wealth he had,
To build a House for Fools and Mad:
And shew'd by one satyric Touch,
No Nation wanted it so much...

– Jonathan Swift: *Verses on the Death of*
Doctor Swift

In St. Patrick's Hospital, founded in 1747 with funds bequeathed by the great satirist Jonathan Swift, the first step was to sedate me and feed me up. During the second day a young woman came to my bedside, introducing herself as my counsellor Regina ('with a hard *g*, please').

'How do you feel today?'

'Not too bad. How soon can I leave?'

'You've only just arrived. We have a lot to talk about when you're feeling up to it, so be patient.'

My tactless question had escaped me involuntarily; in fact I had no objections to being patient. By now I was at last open to listening to what others had to say, and willing to concede that they might know what they were talking about.

One of these others was Rolande, a counsellor in charge of the so-called 'Reality' discussion group. When I first nervously participated, he asked me for my views as to why I drank too much.

'Well, I'm an artist, and I don't have a nine-to-five job. That means I can drink as much as I like whenever I like without having to answer to a boss. It also means I have a lot of time to brood, and maybe that has made me extra sensitive...'

Rolande's riposte was merciless.

'You're obviously an intelligent fellow – I know that you even have a university degree. But I hope you realise that what you've just said is unbelievably stupid!'

For a moment I was startled and resentful and thought of walking out of the room, but that reflex passed and I smiled feebly.

'OK. Please tell me why it's unbelievably stupid.'

And he did, and I listened.

Something had changed. The reflexes that had blocked insight down the years were still there, but they were ghosts of themselves and evaporated one by one. I soon came to like and respect Regina and saw Rolande as a reliable guide to this unfamiliar new world.

The question 'why did you drink too much?' was aimed at exposing my delusions rather than ferreting out the possible causes of my addiction. In St. Patrick's, questions of causation were relegated to the background in favour of a constructive critique of patients' defence mechanisms. The disease model of alcoholism, favoured by A.A., was largely accepted but patients were discouraged from using it as an alibi to shirk responsibility for their own actions. A.A.'s 'twelve steps' were presented as a useful set of guiding principles for recovery, but not as dogmas; the 'higher power' was mentioned, a notion to which I had an instinctive resistance, but it was stressed that it could be interpreted in a non-religious way.

I resolved for the time being to live with these ideas without dissecting them. The causes of my addiction were less important than the necessity to overcome it here and now. I had accepted that I had no control over my drinking, and was prepared to defer in all things to people like Rolande and Regina. That the higher power was so down-to-earth invested it with some authority.

The plan was that I should remain in St. Pat's (to give it its affectionate nickname) for five weeks. Unfortunately, my health insurance company found a loophole: it was less than twelve months since it had covered my stay in St. Vincent's, so it was not liable to cover my present treatment. After two weeks, paid for by my father from his depleted pension, I was obliged to leave. It was agreed that I would visit as a daily out-patient for the next three months, and by special arrangement I would be given my lunch there on weekdays.

In the afternoon of 1 July 1988 I left St. Patrick's and walked back to Pembroke Street. The weather was fine, and I felt well. Had I been asked, I would not have said that I felt optimistic or confident about the future, nor would I have expressed a de-termination never to drink again: these issues simply did not arise. The phrase 'one day at a time' (which I had often paro-died as 'one pint at a time') had imprinted itself on my brain, and no longer even struck me as a cliché: it was something as self-evident as the desirability of eating when hungry or look-ing right and left when crossing a busy street.

Using a scissors and a blunt razor, I shaved off the ratty beard that had disfigured me for months. The face that looked back from the mirror was scratched and bleeding, a little gaunt, but fascinating. It was both the face of a friend who had long vanished from view, and that of a strange new self in the process of formation.

I knocked on the door of my landlord's office. He was barely polite at first, but I gave him no time to deliver a well-deserved lecture. I told him that I would not be able to pay him what I owed him until I had a talk with my bank manager. This could not happen until the following week (it was now Friday eve-ning) but I guaranteed that he would get back every penny and would never have such problems with me again.

The crusty solicitor from Ulster frowned and looked hard into my eyes. He saw something there, and sighed.

'Very well – I believe you. I'll see you next week.'

Next morning I travelled to visit my father. He had sold the house in Bunclody and was now living in the Community Village in Carnew, County Wicklow. Here he had a small house to himself; for all his complaints about his 'elderly' neighbours, most if not all of whom were younger than himself, he had achieved a degree of semi-contented resignation.

I stepped off the bus in Bunclody, eight miles from Carnew, and was met by my father as so often in the past. The difference was that I had no fear of his smelling alcohol from my breath, nor would I have to spend the weekend enduring cold turkey. Over the next two days we talked little but enjoyed one another's company, taking turns to cook, eating unhealthy quantities of potato crisps between meals, watching television, and sitting side by side, each immersed in a book. I told him frankly about my financial problems, explaining that I would need to pay the landlord on Monday morning. I asked him to lend me the money and stressed that this would really and truly be a loan, to be repaid when next I visited. He gave me the money without hesitation.

And I did indeed repay him. In establishing a new relationship with my father in the final years of his life, I could feel that I had to some degree atoned for the cruel accusation I had thrown in his face one summer's night fifteen years earlier.

I returned to Dublin, paid off the landlord, and visited my bank manager. Although my *cnuas* had not yet arrived, although I had overdrawn my account, although I had used an obsolete banking card after my current one had been confiscated, I asked him to lend me some more money. He looked at me quizzically, saw something in my eyes, and complied.

And now my life resumed, without fanfare, and with re-markably little difficulty. Each morning I walked to St. Pat's, attended meetings and lectures, spoke with Regina, had lunch and walked home. I attended A.A. meetings in TCD, a disci-pline I maintained for more than two years, only relinquishing it with my counsellor's consent.

I re-established links with my brother John and his wife Ursula, and with friends and colleagues from the music world. I still occasionally visited Grogans, drinking nothing stronger than coffee. Nobody tried to lure me off the wagon, perhaps seeing in my eyes the same determination others had noticed. I paid off my slate, and repaid as many of my other debts as possible (alas, alcoholics acquire many debts that outlive their creditors).

For a time I survived on a pittance, supplementing my lunches at St. Pat's with processed cheese, digestive biscuits, and Bovril. A packet of potato crisps, divided up over an entire day, served as an occasional treat.

I had one advantage over recovering alcoholics who are faced with the daunting project of filling a life emptied of al-cohol: all that I had to do was replenish the inner void with everything that I had scraped out in order to create it. I started listening to classical music again, and for a time found it hard going. It was as if, having somehow betrayed this wonderful art that had offered itself to me when I was still a child, I was not being allowed to enjoy it again without an almost punitive effort.

By the time my October *cnuas* arrived I was able to eman-cipate myself from St. Pat's' canteen, and visit the hospital for lectures just once a week. At first it had seemed that the finan-cial aspect of Aosdána membership might prove the final nail in my coffin, but once I had turned the corner it proved an invaluable support that enabled me to concentrate on recovery without risk of starvation.

In November Bernard Harris of the Contemporary Music Centre organised a public lecture/recital in TCD's music department in which I played and discussed my music for almost two hours. This gruelling event attracted a full house that included fellow composers, painters like Michael Cullen, and writers like Leland Bardwell and Paul Durcan. After this, I felt that I was well and truly back.

The following July, one year sober, a healthy royalty cheque enabled me to visit Patricia in Paris. From there I took a train to Cologne where I stayed with Anette. This time neither of us had unrealistic expectations of what might follow, and neither was disappointed: we were friends, and as we each moved into different relationships that friendship persisted. Later that year we travelled together to Malta; Anette drank cool, refreshing beer and I drank cool refreshing mineral water. Each of us was satisfied.

Patricia invested in a small studio apartment off the Avenue de Clichy in Paris, and this became my occasional refuge until she sold it again in 1993. Our father died in 1991, leaving me a small bequest with which I secured a mortgage and bought a cottage in Sligo. That year I was featured composer (alongside the Hungarian György Kúrtag) in Dublin's second *Accents* festival, at which roughly one-third of my entire output to date was performed. The festival began with my Dublin Millennium orchestral piece *Thresholds*; I gave a piano recital myself, but mostly I listened critically and concluded that, as a composer, I did not have too much to be ashamed of.

In 1992 *Death of a Medium* was published, the mock-gothic novel I had begun in Oldenburg. It was a critical success, even if it sold relatively few copies, and it has continued to lead a cultish, subterranean existence ever since.

I developed an interest in politics and eventually became involved in a number of campaigns advocating solidarity with the victims of oppression. In this way, as I have suggested, my early experience of bullying was at last being positively recycled.

In 1995 I began a relationship with the German woman called Renate whom I had unjustly dismissed as 'a stuck-up prig' when she failed to be impressed by my suicide scars sixteen years earlier. Today we live together in central Dublin, not far from Leeson Street and Pembroke Street where so many of the scenes of my alcoholic drama had been acted out.

ﺵ   ﺵ   ﺵ

Abstention from drink taught me that what I had taken for my depressiveness was an effect rather than a cause of alcohol abuse. It taught me that while I was indeed 'a loner', as my medical records from St. Vincent's had claimed, I was not really a lonely person but someone whose inner resources disposed him to enjoy solitude. I also enjoyed good company, and gradually began to forge and rebuild friendships unconnected to alcohol. People saw me as someone whose ghost had lived among them for many years, and greeted me as if I had never been absent.

Contrary to appearances, I had never really been a compulsive drinker; I could spend weeks with my parents without feeling the need for a pint or a short. That need returned on the resumption of drinking. My real compulsion was to surrender self-control, and this psychological urge brought physical compulsion in its train.

Clearly, at some point I came to fit the classic pattern of 'low self-esteem plus big ego'. So what was the source of my low self-esteem? Perhaps this memoir has provided some evidence from which readers may draw their own conclusions. I would also remind the detective of that sinister fetish: the straightened coat hanger. The terror of responsibility was also, in part, the terror of becoming an adult and dealing with adult things.

In my reading around the subject of alcoholism, I have been struck by the psychoanalytic concept of 'narcissistic mortification'. Psychoanalysts link it to the child's early fantasies of omnipotence which cannot survive life's inevitable assaults. Mortification (the first syllable of which evokes death) is the dread of losing one's identity, a form of 'annihilation anxiety' reminiscent of the helplessness of infancy. Terror, fright, dread, overwhelmed helplessness, childish fantasies of omnipotence inevitably demolished by life, the embrace of humiliation as an irrational reaction to past bullying... Each element of this litany can be traced in the course of this memoir. Whether this fully explains why I drank to excess is doubtful, but then, and perhaps fortunately, not every human peculiarity admits of full explanation.

Eventually mortification may modulate into shame, an unpleasant emotion but one that can provide a sharp stimulus to change one's behaviour. The transition towards recovery may also be helped by the process known as 'maturing out', whereby with advancing years addicts simply tire of their addictions. This 'maturing out' can happen earlier or later in life. It is not necessary for drinkers to wait until they have hit rock bottom in order to emerge from the nightmare of alcoholism. As a curate in San Francisco, my late brother Declan was forced by his superiors to spend several months in a rehabilitation centre; the treatment 'took', and he spent the last decades of his life in productive sobriety. He would, by his own account, tell those to whom he ministered that, 'I have never come across a hopeless case, except maybe once'. I was the exception, yet in the end I was not.

In fact I was repeatedly on the brink of emerging from my sodden Purgatory, but was plunged back into it by my own delusions. Perhaps it is it possible that, had I encountered a Regina or a Rolande and received appropriate treatment at an earlier stage, I and those on whom my behaviour impinged might have been spared years of misery and aggravation. Or perhaps I had encountered such people and refused to recognise them.

Alcoholics Anonymous promises the sober alcoholic 'a life beyond your wildest dreams'. The wildest dream of the person caught in the snare of addiction is not fame or prosperity, but simple normality with its everyday frustrations and satisfactions. Once such a state has been achieved, it is very easy to take it for granted and suppress all memory of previous horrors. The other extreme, of course, is a constant brooding on the past, and on what might have been had other paths been chosen. It is important to remember and to be eternally vigilant – but not to be crippled by mortification.

I have a temperamental inclination towards pessimism, even fatalism. Rationally, however, the course of my own life would seem to contradict such a tendency. For this reason I am wary about the political slogan 'pessimism of the intellect, optimism of the will'; when pessimism proves to have been unfounded it is intellectually irresponsible to persist in it. The same goes for fatalism. My brother Declan's conviction that I was 'a hopeless case' would have been proved correct had one of my suicide attempts been successful. The only reason that I survived them was because my physical constitution was so resilient – but survive them I did, and lived to outgrow the mental habits that had precipitated them.

I cannot offer the active alcoholic any advice on how to conquer their addiction, beyond the injunction: seek help, and accept it with humility. However, I can bear witness to the fact that I find life as a survivor well worth living, despite – and perhaps because of – its frustrations, dead ends and moments of near despair. The active alcoholic cannot imagine this, because their imagination is literally bottled in. Not to take the leap of trust and accept that things may be otherwise is unfair to oneself. Experiences such as mine, after all, are far from unique.

This brings to mind another political slogan, dear to those of us dedicated to apparently hopeless causes: 'a different world is possible'. And why not, since a different life is possible.